THE

UPANISHADS

THE

UPANISHADS

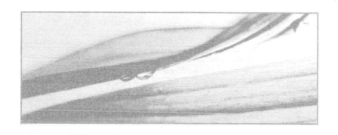

Selections translated by
ALISTAIR SHEARER and **PETER RUSSELL**

Introduced by **ALISTAIR SHEARER**

SACRED TEACHINGS

BELL TOWER NEW YORK

Published by Bell Tower, New York, New York.
Member of the Crown Publishing Group,
a division of Random House, Inc.
www.randomhouse.com

Bell Tower and colophon are registered trademarks of
Random House, Inc.

Originally published, in different form, by Wildwood House
Limited, London, in 1978, subsequently in the United States
by HarperCollins, New York, in 1979, and reissued by Unwin
Hyman, London, in 1989.

Printed in the United States of America

DESIGN BY BARBARA STURMAN

Library of Congress Cataloging-in-Publication Data
Upanishads. English. Selections.
    The Upanishads selections / translated by Alistair Shearer and
Peter Russell ; introduced by Alistair Shearer.
    I. Shearer, Alistair. II. Russell, Peter. III. Title.
    BL1124.52 .E5   2002
    294.5'9218—dc21   2002003946

ISBN 0-609-61107-0

10 9 8 7 6 5 4 3 2 1

First Bell Tower Edition 2003

CONTENTS

6

◉

CONTENTS

OUR PRIMARY DEBT of thanks is to our teacher, Maharishi Mahesh Yogi, a living Upanishadic sage who has sown so many subtle seeds for the transformation of world consciousness. All that is of worth in this book is due to what we have understood of his teaching.

Heartfelt thanks are also due to Toinette Lippe, who has been responsible for so much good in the world of publishing. She had the farsightedness to republish this translation and worked so hard to make the project a reality.

ACKNOWLEDGMENTS

ONE BRIGHT MAY MORNING at the end of the 1960s, a friend, Peter Russell, came round to my rooms in Cambridge to lend me a small book with a black-and-white cover. It was entitled *The Science of Being and Art of Living* and was written by Maharishi Mahesh Yogi, whose technique of Transcendental Meditation, or TM, was then all the rage. I tried to read the book but couldn't get into it. Nevertheless, something drew me to try the meditation itself. A couple of weeks later, in a room full of stillness and the scent of freesias, I learned the simple technique. Little did I realize then that I had taken the first step on a lifelong spiritual journey.

Some years later, Peter and I met up again. Our lives had developed in different ways. He had gone on from a degree in physics to take degrees in computer science and psychology and had published his first book; I had got married, received a postgraduate degree in Sanskrit, and was lecturing on Oriental art and architecture. But both of us had continued with TM, spent time with Maharishi, and become teachers of the technique, and both of us continued to be fascinated by the possibilities it offered to expand awareness and improve daily life. We decided to combine our different perspectives and work together on a new translation of key passages from the Upanishads—ancient Sanskrit texts central to the spiritual tradition from which the TM technique comes. This book is the result.

Our aim was to make comprehensible to the modern reader what had previously been held to be almost impossibly recondite works of philosophy. Youthful presumption, perhaps, but we were inspired by the way in which Maharishi's teachings had opened up the beginnings of the spiritual life to hundreds of thousands of ordinary, practical people immersed in ordinary, practical lives. And, ambitious though it was, our attempt could not have wholly obscured the profundity of the original. People loved the book. The first edition, illustrated with black-and-white images by the masterly photographer Richard Lannoy and designed in the house in Cornwall where D. H. Lawrence once lived, sold well enough to warrant a second.

And now, almost a quarter of a century later, comes this present edition, in smaller format with text standing alone. In some ways the world has changed enormously, but those social and spiritual concerns that so galvanized our sixties generation have not faded out of fashion along with the lurid floral shirts and crushed velvet trousers. In fact, their relevance becomes more pressing each year. Underpinning specific contemporary concerns—terrorism, genetic engineering, the environment, globalization—aches a general realization that we have lost our way.

Each day it becomes clearer that the glib promises held out by scientific materialism and the free market will not suffice to heal the heart, order the mind, and restore in us that compassion and nobility of purpose which befits our species and our destiny.

And this is where the perennial wisdom of the Upanishads comes in. Now, more than ever, these ancient texts offer invaluable education in what is our true evolutionary priority—the development of the unused cosmic potential that resides in each and every one of us. This latent spiritual intelligence is our human birthright, waiting to be uncovered. It is the one tool that is indispensable if we are to solve our manifold problems. The fruit of this intelligence is the realization that we are one Self. Unless we begin to live this reality, our future is bleak indeed.

ALISTAIR SHEARER

Hail the voice of the Bard!
Who Present, Past and Future, sees;
Whose ears have heard
The Holy Word
That walked among the ancient trees . . .

Introduction to "Songs of Experience"
by William Blake

IF YOU SEARCH for the Upanishads in a bookstore or on the Net, you will probably be directed to a section marked "Indian philosophy." This unfortunate pigeonholing is doubly inaccurate, as, strictly speaking, the Upanishads are neither "Indian" nor "philosophy." Their teachings are universal, no more Indian knowledge than $E=mc^2$ is German-Jewish physics. Nor are they "philosophy" in the conventional sense of being the hard-thought conclusions of professional thinkers, who, despite—or perhaps because of—all their intellectual striving, rarely exemplify the dictionary definition of the philosopher as one who is "wise, calm, and temperate."

Certainly, like any philosophers, the sages of the Upanishads were concerned with finding Truth, but they realized that as all experience is, and always must be, mediated through the mind, knowledge of the outside world can only go as far as the knower has knowledge of himself. Moreover, they considered our normal waking state of consciousness too limited and too unstable to comprehend any ultimate reality, for as Truth is that which does not change, it demands an equally unchanging consciousness to appreciate it. So their interest was to transcend the ostensibly rational processes by which we normally try to make sense of the world and reach a state of pure Being, which, lying beyond all thinking and feeling, is the very basis of the mind. They called this state the Self and, as it is unchanging and impartial, considered it the only reliable basis for true understanding of both inner and outer reality. To live in this state of expanded awareness is to be enlightened, and thus the Upanishadic ideal agrees with the ancient Greek definition of true philosophy as *gnosis,* the cultivation of sacred wisdom. The sage of the Upanishads embodied Plato's vision of the

Philosopher King as described in the *Phaedrus*: an enlightened being who would "live in constant companionship with the divine order of the world."

Are the Upanishads poetry, then? Yes, if we understand poetry in its highest sense, as the inspired use of sound to transform awareness and unlock the door to the infinite. The Upanishads are the distillation of a timeless wisdom that, to protect itself, was transmitted orally from generation to generation, as sacred knowledge always has been. (Those cultures that first developed writing, such as Sumeria and ancient China, did so primarily to record commercial transactions, never to transmit priestly knowledge.) This perennial wisdom is known as the Vedic tradition of knowledge. Its medium was Vedic, the sacred language par excellence, believed to be not merely a conventional system of representation based on linear logic but the language of nature herself, composed of the primordial sounds that promote order in the evolving universe. These sounds, like music, communicate preverbally and have a universal meaning that transcends all cultural boundaries; they nourish and purify the physiology and thrill the soul.

The nearest spoken language to Vedic is Sanskrit, oldest of the Indo-European tongues, and it is in their Sanskrit form that the Upanishads have come down to us. The recondite complexities of Vedic knowledge have concealed its deeper meaning from Western scholars, who, not being born into the tradition, have almost without exception failed to plumb its depths. As the recorded Vedic material predates the Old Testament by at least two thousand years, academics have assumed its elaborate abstractions and symbolic cosmologies to be a primitive and inchoate articulation of the religious impulse. Nothing could be further from the truth.

According to this teaching, the ground of all being is an infinite and unified field of Consciousness, eternal and self-luminous. This Consciousness creates the universe from its own depths, by reverberating within itself. These reverberations generate sound, and this sound, the vibrations of the first sprouting of the absolute field of intelligence that underlies and pervades everything, is called Veda. Thus, Veda is said to be the source of creation; it is the DNA of the universe, containing all manifest possibilities in seed form. These possibilities, the impulses of creative intelligence latent in the very nature of the absolute Consciousness, unfold in an orderly and sequential manner as the same laws of nature time after time, cosmic cycle after cycle, to structure life. To find the nearest equivalent of this abstract view in Western thought, we must again look to the ancient Greeks. Their concept of *logos*, synonymous with Veda, was adopted by early Christian theology as the divine "Word," celebrated in the well-known opening verses of St. John's gospel: "In the beginning was the Word, and the Word was with God, and the Word was God." According to Vedic understanding, however, this process is not confined to a historical beginning at a particular point in time. "The beginning" is ongoing, as the eternal unfolding of the Natural Law that governs the universe, moment to moment. In theological terms it is the continuous and invincible enactment of the will of God.

So the Veda, in the highest sense, is not a collection of scriptures sitting on a dusty shelf in some temple or library but the pulsation of life itself, taking place in the depths of our own being to structure our minds and bodies. Made in the image of God, with our uniquely developed brain and nervous system, we are the prime example of "the Holy Word" made flesh. One whose awareness is pure enough to cognize these sounds directly is known as a seer (*rishi*), and it is from the cognitions of such seers that the entire Vedic teaching, including the Upanishads, has been revealed.

The Sanskrit word for poet is *kāvi* ("maker"), and the Vedic poet was a bard who, as in Blake's quote above, could see the present, past, and future because his awareness was rooted in the infinite depth of the present moment, in touch with the transcendental field that lies beyond time. Such a bard is a seer whose utterances, flowing from the very cusp of experience, resonate with divine power, as did Adam's words in Eden, when his God-given gift of naming the animals conferred authority over them. Indeed, such a seer is himself an Adam, first of men; with his mind stationed at the source of creation, he is at one with the inexhaustible freshness of the endlessly dawning light.

The primary power of the Upanishads lies in the effect their sound vibrations have on the nervous system. It is not even necessary for the hearer to understand the meaning of these sounds to receive their beneficial influence. Any writing down is obviously a considerable loss of this power; any translation even more so. Nor is this loss mitigated when the language is English, for despite having by far the largest vocabulary of any language, English is impoverished just where Sanskrit is richest: in terms that succinctly describe finely nuanced levels of expanded awareness and the realities such states reveal. Not least of the problems this poses to any translator is how to differentiate the various modes of the ultimate Consciousness that is beyond all naming and to which the Upanishads return again and again. Following the texts (and overcoming a modern disinclination toward capital letters), we have tried to adopt a consistent scheme in describing this beatitude. As the limitless ground of the individual, it is called the Self; as the adorable and radiant presence creating the world, it is the Divine; as the intelligence that organizes and administers creation, it is Consciousness; as the unmoving matrix from and in which the many relative worlds of time, space, and causation evolve, it is the Absolute. And when this Reality is described as one wholeness, the unified totality of its two complementary aspects—silence and dynamism, spirit and matter—we have retained the Sanskrit term *brahman* because there is simply no equivalent in English.

Previous translations of the Upanishads have generally fallen into one of two camps. The academic versions produced by scholars such as Sarvapelli Radhakrishnan, Ernest Hume, and Swami Nikhilananda follow the letter of the originals but all too often miss the liveliness of their spirit, and so they tend to come across to the modern reader as rather dry and distanced. On the other hand, the poetic renderings by writers such as W. B. Yeats and Purohit Swami, or Juan Mascaro, tend to sacrifice philosophical accuracy in favor of lyrical feeling. In this present translation, we have tried to steer a middle course between these two approaches and present what is actually a very precise body of teachings in a form that is both accessible and relevant to contemporary life.

The word *sanskrit* means literally "that which has been adorned, decorated, or transformed" and is usually translated as the "perfected." Remaining virtually unchanged for over three thousand years (compare, for example, English!), it has given cohesion to India's incorrigible cultural variety, much as Latin once did in Europe. Proficiency in Sanskrit has always been considered a sacred accomplishment. Like many ancient languages, it has a logical, almost mathematical structure. Each word is divisible into component parts, most of which can in turn be traced to one of several hundred verbal roots. These roots, monosyllabic sounds representing general qualities of action, are said to embody, as well as signify, the basic energies of the universe. Analysis of a Sanskrit word or idea thus draws us from the expressed world of multiplicity to a more fundamental and causal level, the field of the root, and the concrete world of thought and action is seen to stem from a more abstract one. Sanskrit serves as the mediator between this hidden, causal area of potential and the manifest realm of a particular name, form, and function.

The worldview that shaped Sanskrit was a holistic one, and the language reflects this breadth of vision. Objects are defined in terms of their function; actors and actions are seen as interrelated parts of a greater whole. Many terms, both abstract and concrete, reflect the fact that manifestation is the play of dualities that are complementary. For example: The word for world is *jagat,* which, coming from the root *GAM,* "to go," means "that which goes, moves, changes." This not only conveys the essential nature of relative life—its impermanence—and hints at its evolutionary dynamism but also implies that there is something that does *not* change or move, a constant against which life's impermanence can be contrasted. Thus, implicit in the concept of the relative world is its unchanging backdrop: the Absolute. Such resonance in an apparently commonplace term evinces a subtlety quite missing in the English equivalent.

Although stable historically, Sanskrit is very fluid in usage. The same word may have different

meanings and can sometimes even take opposite
meanings, depending on the context; nouns and
adjectives can be interchangeable and verbs are
often omitted as understood. Philosophical Sanskrit
is extremely aphoristic; one word in the original
usually needs several English words to render it
correctly—sometimes even a paragraph! Added to
this, Indian tradition often analyzes words symbolically rather than grammatically. Each syllabic sound
is given its own meaning, and thus the interpretation
of a word when taken as a combination of symbolic
syllables may soar way beyond its literal significance.

This interactive liveliness, demanding an ever
fresh response from the reader, characterizes Sanskrit
as the archetypical sacred language, ideally suited to
encapsulate multiple associations that convey different levels of meaning to different eyes. A word or
passage may be interpreted in a variety of ways, none
of which need exclude the others. Thus, the same text
could be understood as a slice of history, a myth, a
psychological treatise, or a spiritual discourse—or
any combination of these. To allow their various
levels space to emerge, the Upanishads should be
quietly contemplated rather than just read through;
they will prove salutary yardsticks against which the
fluctuations of our mental clarity can be gauged. On

the other hand, as they stem from an oral tradition, they were composed to be memorized and recited—daily recitation creating conditions in the nervous system suitable to the emergence of the text's inherent spirit. Because of this, they are often repetitive and incantatory, and their power also increases when they are read aloud.

As regards the word *upanishad,* it is derived from the root *SHAD,* meaning "to sit, settle, or approach," together with the prefixes *UPA,* "near," and *NI,* "down." An *upanishad* is thus "a sitting-down-near," and in the India of their composition, no less than today, the seeker of wisdom approached a teacher, sat down at his or her feet, and settled the mind to receive spiritual instruction. Both teacher and pupil had to be well qualified for their relationship. As the Mundaka Upanishad tells us, while the teacher was to be both "learned in the scriptures and established in *brahman*"—in other words, an enlightened being—the pupil was expected to be pure and receptive, "one who is calm and whose mind is quiet." What is required is not an argumentative frame of mind but a mental "settling down"—an *upa-ni-shad*—a turning of the attention inward, away from the constantly changing world of everyday experience toward the silence that lies between, and beyond, our thoughts.

The direct experience of this silence is the gift of meditation, and the practice of meditation has always been central to both the teaching and understanding of these texts. Ultimately, the Upanishads celebrate an ecstasy that transcends thought and the workings of the intellect. And as this realm is beyond words, any attempt to describe it must at best be "a near approach"—an *upanishad*.

In our translation we have been primarily concerned with presenting an introduction to some of the basic tenets of the Vedic teaching. As far as possible in letting the texts speak for themselves, we have focused on nine of the most important Upanishads, three in their entirety, six in part. The choice of texts and the order of their presentation have been decided by our desire to let the teaching unfold in as logical manner as possible, thereby introducing the reader step-by-step to a knowledge unparalleled in its profundity and importance.

ALISTAIR SHEARER

OM

That, the eternal realm of the Absolute, is full;

This, the transitory realm of the relative, is full.

From the fullness of one emerges the fullness of the other;

Fullness coming from fullness, yet a single Fullness still remains.

THE

UPANISHADS

Māndūkya Upanishad

SEVERAL MILLENNIA before the beginning
of the Christian era, the sages of the Upanishads
formulated a phenomenology that was extraordi-
narily profound, simple, and elegant. They identified
four major states of consciousness, each of which,
as modern science has shown, has its own distinct
mode of physiological functioning, and each of
which gives us a very different experience of reality.
The first three—waking, dreaming, and sleeping—
are familiar to all of us; indeed, we spend our
lives passing continually from one of these states
to another without giving it a second thought.
Underlying and obscured by these three states,
however, is a hidden substratum of constant
awareness. When emphasizing the distinction
between this continuum and the three transitory
states, the Upanishads refer to it simply as "the
fourth"; when describing it as our immortal essence,
it is known as the Self. This unbroken awareness
is transcendental—beyond time, space, and
causation. It is the ultimate reality of life.

When "the fourth" is lived continuously alongside the other three states coming and going as before, there is Enlightenment. This is not just a mood of feeling good in the waking state but an entirely different level of consciousness, with its own physiology and its own reality. Enlightenment is as different from waking as waking is from dreaming.

In the dreaming state the sages included not only the activity we recognize by that name but any subjectively absorbed experience where "the attention dwells within, charmed by the mind's subtler creations." Into this category, therefore, fall many experiences that are often considered spiritual, such as mediumistic trance, astral travel, and inner visions and voices. But as the Māndūkya Upanishad implies, such experiences are not in fact spiritual, merely subtle. The spirit lies beyond any experience, no matter how unusual or glamorous.

Dreamless sleep, being devoid of the boundaries imposed by time, space, and the limited sense of "I," is said in the texts to be the nearest approximation most of us ever get to knowing our true nature! In Enlightenment, however, this usually unconscious blankness is "experienced as an ocean of silence and bliss." This is because when awareness of the Self is permanently established, it is not lost even when the body and mind are sleeping. But if the mind is asleep, how can there be awareness of anything? Here we must understand the crucial distinction the Upanishads make between "mind" and "Self." They teach that it is the latter that is the source of conscious awareness, and this consciousness is, in its pure nature, universal. The former, with all its perceptions, thoughts, and feelings, is not the source of consciousness but its localized and individual reflector. This distinction is made most tellingly by Patanjali, in his *Yoga Sūtras* (c. second century C.E.), the most seminal work on yoga. In four crucial verses (4.17–20) he describes the relationship of mind and Self: "An object is experienced only when it colors the mind. But the mind itself is always experienced because it is witnessed by the unchanging Self. The mind does not shine by its own light. It too is an object, illumined by the Self. Not being self-luminous, the mind cannot be aware of itself and its object at the same time." Thus, waking, dreaming, and sleeping are the temporary modes of the mind that come and go in the unwavering light of pure consciousness. The Self is not the contents of the mind any more than a beam of light is the object it illuminates. It is the impartial and unattached witness of all that takes place, rendering perceptible the fluctuations of the mind, functioning of the body, and happenings of the outside world, but forever free of them and their changes.

As the Self is our own deepest nature, contact with it is quite natural. It will occur whenever the mind, focusing through one of the five senses, experiences its object at increasingly fine levels until the finest has been transcended. Then the individual mind no longer exists, and the Self, the light of consciousness, is left alone by itself. As long as the attention is sufficiently relaxed, this can happen quite spontaneously. Many people have had the experience—perhaps when listening to music, watching a beautiful sunset, or making love—and its effect is always life-enhancing, sometimes bringing about a complete change of attitude. It has been recorded particularly often among artists, poets, and mystics.

The opening to this transcendental reality is the living fountainhead of all religions. In itself prior to doctrine, dogma, or division, the experience will be named and interpreted according to its cultural setting. The Buddha, a very practical teacher who taught in terms of phenomenal realism, called it *nirvāna,* a term meaning "the extinction of suffering."

Later Buddhist schools developed different epithets for pure consciousness according to their various perspectives, describing it philosophically as "Emptiness," psychologically as "Mind," or ontologically as the "Buddha-nature" inherent in everything. Zen teachers, ever pragmatic, called it "no-mind" to emphasize that it lies beyond all concepts. In the very different cultural ambience of the Semitic faiths, Jewish mystics praised the Self as the radiant indwelling Shekhinah, and Islamic Sufis adored it as "the Beloved," while the fourteenth-century German monk Meister Eckhart preached of it as "the desert beyond God." Six hundred years later, the scholar and mystic Thomas Merton described the Self as "the infinite *I am* which is the very name of the Almighty." Examples such as these are legion, found in all the world's faiths.

The technique of merging the mind in the Self is what the East calls "meditation" and the West, "contemplation." Practiced regularly, it brings about the settled state (*samādhi*) when the individual thinking mind has become quite silent but awareness still remains. In the boundless gap between two thoughts, individual mind comes to rest and, due to the inherently self-referring nature of consciousness, which can be aware of itself without entertaining any external object, the Self knows itself. Following the Māndūkya Upanishad's classification of the four states, we could say that *samādhi* is sleep in the waking state! Only when all the mental activity—perceptions, thoughts, feelings—that habitually obscures its native luminosity has ceased can the Self shine forth. As our text says, "It is known only by becoming It."

The medium of meditation recommended in the Upanishads is sound or *mantra,* and this for several reasons. Hearing is the subtlest of the five senses; it is the first to awaken in the fetus and the last to leave the body at death, as the wisdom traditions recognized by reading sacred texts to the dying or recently dead. Thought, our most constant and intimate companion, is internalized sound. And as the physical vibrations of sound are the least impeded, the effects of thinking a mantra will spontaneously nourish not only the person who meditates but his or her environment as well.

Sound, moreover, is the creative energy of the Absolute, for it is through the power of cosmic sound that the universe is being continuously created, moment to moment: Matter is energy; energy is vibration; vibration is sound. When the divine intelligence begins to stir, its infinite nature moves to a point in a sprouting of hitherto unexpressed potential. This movement generates a jungle of undifferentiated sound, a collected mass of humming frequencies before the specific strands of vibration begin to separate out to shape the world of relativity that the Upanishads call "name and form." This mass of frequencies generalizes as the primordial vibration OM, the alpha and omega of Vedic wisdom, so powerful in leading the mind back to its undifferentiated source that it is warned only recluses should meditate on it.

The Māndūkya Upanishad is a very highly revered text; the Muktika Upanishad claims that, correctly understood, it can lead directly to liberation. Part of its reputation is due to the celebrated commentary appended by the great sage Gaudapāda. Appealing only to reason, rather than traditional scriptural authority, he establishes the immaculate singularity of the Self, unrelated to and unsupported by anything else, yet the basis of all. "It is unborn, ever awake, free from illusion, having no form or name. It is one and continuous, all-knowing. There is no metaphor whatever in saying this." Gaudapāda systematized his teaching of the Self in the philosophy of non-dualism known as Advaita Vedānta, the zenith of Indian spirituality, made universally famous by his illustrious successor, Ādi Shankara.

OM,
The imperishable sound, is the seed of all that exists.
The past, the present, the future—all are but the
    unfolding of OM.
And whatever transcends the three realms of time,
    that indeed is the flowering of OM.

This whole creation is ultimately *brahman*.
And the Self, this also is *brahman*.

This pure Self has four aspects:

The first is the waking state,
This is the experience of the reality common to
    everyone, when the attention faces outwards,
    enjoying the world in all its variety.

The second is experience of subjective worlds, such
    as in dreaming.
Here the attention dwells within, charmed by the
    mind's subtler creations.

The third is deep sleep.

The mind rests, with awareness suspended.

This state beyond duality—from which the waves of
thinking emerge—is enjoyed by the enlightened
as an ocean of silence and bliss.

The fourth, say the wise, is the pure Self, alone.

Dwelling in the heart of all, It is the lord of all, the
seer of all, the source and goal of all.

It is not outer awareness, It is not inner awareness,
nor is It a suspension of awareness.

It is not knowing, It is not unknowing, nor is It
knowingness itself.

It can neither be seen nor understood.

It cannot be given boundaries.

It is ineffable and beyond thought.

It is indefinable.

It is known only through becoming It.

It is the end of all activity, silent and unchanging,
the supreme good, one without a second.

It is the real Self.

It, above all, should be known.

This pure Self and OM are as one; and the different
aspects of the Self correspond to OM and its
constituent sounds, A-U-M.

Experience of the outer world corresponds to A,
the first sound.
This initiates action and achievement.
Whoever awakens to this acts in freedom and
achieves success.

Experience of the inner world corresponds to U,
the second sound.
This initiates upholding and unification.
Whoever awakens to this upholds the tradition of
knowledge and unifies the diversities of life.
Everything that arises speaks to him of *brahman*.

The state of dreamless sleep corresponds to M,
the third sound.
This initiates measurement and merging.
Whoever awakens to this merges with the world yet
has the measure of all things.

The pure Self alone, that which is indivisible, which
cannot be described, the supreme good, the one
without a second, that corresponds to the
wholeness of OM.
Whoever awakens to that becomes the Self.

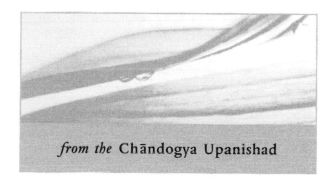

from the Chāndogya Upanishad

LIFE IN VEDIC TIMES was divided into four stages. First came the education of the celibate student who studied sacred knowledge for twelve or fourteen years as a foundation for life; this was followed by the busy life of the householder involved in work, family, and worldly commitments. Then came the period of the forest-dweller who retired from overly active engagement in the world to devote more time to the spiritual life. The last stage, for those who were suited to it, was that of the renunciate sage who, living off alms, wandered and taught throughout the land. While it is impossible to say how widely this ideal was actually followed in ancient times, even three thousand years later its vestiges can still be seen in Indian society, and for all of us it remains a generally appropriate pattern that can give shape and meaning to human life.

In what is one of the simplest and most loved of Upanishadic stories, the brahmin youth Shvetaketu returns home after completing the first life stage to encounter the unexpected wisdom of his father.

As the young man discovers, what is often needed in the acquisition of true understanding is the humility to undergo a process of unlearning.

Shvetaketu's father instructs his son by leading him through varied examples of his ultimate identity with the universal Self. The repeated phrase "You are That" is one of the "four great sayings" by which the Master traditionally lifts the student who is ripe into the state of Enlightenment.

Once upon a time there lived a young boy called
Shvetaketu ("White Star"), the son of Uddālaka
Āruna. One day his father said to him, "My son,
you are now twelve and the time has come for you
to go and study the sacred teachings, for it is the
tradition in our family that everyone should study
the Vedas and become a true brahmin."

When he was twenty-four, Shvetaketu returned
home, having studied all the Vedas. He was full
of conceit and arrogantly thought he knew everything.

"Shvetaketu," his father said, "you are conceited
and arrogant and think yourself well read, but did
you ever ask for that knowledge by which one hears
that which cannot be heard, sees that which cannot
be seen, and knows that which cannot be known?"

"Whatever is that teaching, sir?" the son inquired.

"Very well, my son. By knowing one lump of
clay, you know the essence of all things made of clay,
their differences being only in name and form. By
knowing one nugget of gold, you know the essence
of all things made of gold, their differences being
only in name and form. By knowing one piece of

iron, you know the essence of all things made of iron, their differences being only in name and form. In the same way, my son, through this knowledge you gain the essence of all knowledges."

"My venerable teachers could not have known of this, for if they had they would surely have passed it on to me. So could you, dear father, teach me?" Shvetaketu asked.

"Very well, my son. In the beginning there was pure Being, one without a second. Some people, however, believe that in the beginning there was only non-Being, one without a second, and that non-Being gave birth to Being. But how could this be? How could Being arise from non-Being? No, my son, it was pure Being, one without a second, which existed in the beginning.

"Pure Being, thinking to itself: 'May I become many; may I take form,' created light. Light, thinking to itself: 'May I become many; may I take form,' created the ocean of Consciousness. And the ocean of Consciousness, thinking to itself: 'May I become many; may I take form,' created the universe. In this way the whole universe was born from pure Being. And that Being which is the subtlest essence of everything, the supreme reality, the Self of all that exists, YOU ARE THAT, Shvetaketu."

from the CHĀNDOGYA UPANISHAD

"Please, sir, tell me more of this teaching," said the boy.

"Very well, my son. When the bees collect the nectar from many different plants, blending them all into one honey, the individual nectars no longer think: 'I come from this plant,' 'I come from that plant.' In the same way, my son, all creatures when they contact Being lose all awareness of their individual natures. But when they return from Being they regain their individuality. Whether tiger, or lion, or wolf, or boar, or worm, or fly, or gnat, or even mosquito, they become themselves again. Just so, that Being which is the subtlest essence of everything, the supreme reality, the Self of all that exists, YOU ARE THAT, Shvetaketu."

"Please, sir, tell me more of this teaching," said the boy.

"Very well, my son. All rivers, whether they flow to the east or to the west, have arisen from the sea and will return to it again. Yet once these rivers have merged with the sea, they no longer think: 'I am this river,' 'I am that river.' In the same way, my son, all these creatures, when they merge again with Being, do not remember that they originally arose from Being and wound their individual ways through life.

Now that Being which is the subtlest essence of everything, the supreme reality, the Self of all that exists, YOU ARE THAT, Shvetaketu."

"Please, sir, tell me more of this teaching," said the boy.

"Very well, my son. If you were to chop at the root of this great tree, it would bleed but it would not die. If you were to chop at its trunk, it would bleed but it would not die. If you were to chop at its branches, it would bleed but it would not die. Permeated by sap, its life energy, the tree stands firm, drinking and enjoying its nourishment.

"But if the sap withdraws from one of the branches, then that branch withers. If it withdraws from a second branch, then that branch withers. If it withdraws from a third branch, then that branch also withers. If the sap withdraws from the whole tree, then the whole tree withers and dies. In just the same way, my son, when the Self withdraws from the body, the body dies, though the Self lives on. And that Being which is the subtlest essence of everything, the supreme reality, the Self of all that exists, YOU ARE THAT, Shvetaketu."

"Please, sir, tell me more of this teaching," said the boy.

from the CHĀNDOGYA UPANISHAD

"Very well, my son. Go and pick a fig from that tree."

"Here you are, sir."

"Split it open and tell me what you see inside."

"Many tiny seeds, sir."

"Take one of them and split it open and tell me what you see inside."

"Nothing at all, sir."

Then the father said, "The subtlest essence of the fig appears to you as nothing, but, believe me, my son, from that very nothing this mighty tree has arisen. Similarly, that Being which is the subtlest essence of everything, the supreme Self of all that exists, YOU ARE THAT, Shvetaketu."

"Please, sir, tell me more of this teaching," said the boy.

"Very well, my son. Take this salt, put it in a glass of water, and come to me again tomorrow morning."

Shvetaketu did as he was asked, and in the morning his father said to him, "Bring me that salt which you put in the water last night." The boy looked for the salt but could not find it, since it had all dissolved. So the father said, "Take a sip from the top. How does it taste?"

"Salty, sir."

"Pour some away and take a sip from the middle. How does it taste now?"

"Salty, sir."

"Pour some more away and take a sip from the bottom. How does that taste?"

"Still salty, sir."

"Now throw it all away and come here."

The boy did as he was told, saying, "Every drop tasted of salt."

"Similarly, my son, even though you may not perceive pure Being permeating everything, in truth it is there. That Being which is the subtlest essence of everything, the supreme reality, the Self of all that exists, YOU ARE THAT, Shvetaketu."

"Please, sir, tell me more of this teaching," said the boy.

"Very well, my son. Imagine a man who has been blindfolded, led far away from home, and left in the wilderness. He will wander about hopelessly in any direction crying out: 'I have been blindfolded and abandoned here.' But if someone were to remove the blindfold and point out to him the general direction of home, then by using his intelligence he could eventually get there by asking his way from village to village. In just the same way a person who has found a teacher who can show him the right way to liberation knows that he is on the right path and will eventually reach Enlightenment. For that Being which is the subtlest essence of everything, the supreme reality, the Self of all that exists, YOU, SHVETAKETU, ARE THAT."

6.I.1–II.4 and 6.IX.1–XIV.3

Īsha Upanishad

THIS SPARKLING GEM of a text holds a special place in the pantheon of Vedic literature. Traditionally there are said to be 108 Upanishads, of which a dozen or so are principal, and in collections of these, the Īsha Upanishad is generally placed first. Such preeminence is in accordance with the literary tradition whereby the entire content and range of a teaching is contained, in seed form, in its opening. Thus the Īsha Upanishad, although a mere eighteen verses, describes with unmatched lucidity and balance both the path and the goal of all Vedic endeavor—Enlightenment.

Vedic wisdom defines Enlightenment clearly: that state in which the Self is enjoyed at all times, throughout all experience. What, then, is this "Self"? As the Māndūkya Upanishad has intimated, it is not the ego-personality we usually identify with—the limited, mortal "self" conditioned by environment and life experiences and indissolubly associated with the body. Nor is it the "Higher Self," talked of in various New Age teachings, which watches over, advises, and directs us, like some internalized parental, or even godlike, force with whom we can converse. Such intuitions, consoling and nourishing though they may be, stem from unfathomed but still limited levels of our own circumscribed individuality. To the conscious ego they may well appear to be imbued with the mysterious power of the "other," but they are not the transcendental silence of the spirit.

The Self of which the Upanishads teach lies beyond thought, feeling, or archetype. It is the impartial basis of all other aspects of our personal identity and beyond them all. As the unchanging ground of our own consciousness, it is infinite and eternal, the unbounded substratum in which all experience, including that of an individual self or ego, arises. In itself, the Self *does* nothing. It merely *is*. It does not think or perceive or act—these are the functions of our mind and body—it is pure Being, the unattached and immortal vastness from which, and in which, all else takes place. If we want a parallel from a Western tradition, the Self is the eternal: "I am that I am" of the Old Testament.

Yet just as the silent, calm depth of the sea is the basis of all the individual waves that rise and fall, so is this absolute Self the basis of the ever changing relative world of time, space, and causation. The Self vibrates to become the substance of our thoughts and experiences; all the forms and phenomena of the universe are its temporary and nonbinding modifications. This paradoxical situation, whereby the unlimited Divine gives rise to the limited world without compromising its limitless status, is reflected in the language that characterizes the mystical confessions of all religions and is a feature of this particular text.

In our normal state of awareness, which the Upanishads call "ignorance," we look outward from a fixed center we call "I" and see a world of differences existing separately from ourselves. The enlightened perspective, on the other hand, sees all phenomena as projections of the endless spaciousness of the Self, which is our true nature. The locus of awareness has now shifted from the boundaries of a limited personality to the expansiveness of an all-inclusive field, not localized to the body, in which all phenomena arise, inhere, and eventually pass away. The typical person thinks he exists "within" his body and that his body exists "in" the world; the enlightened experience that not only the body, but the entire world exists in them, as fluctuations of the Self.

To describe the view that results from such a radical turnaround in consciousness, we must stand conventional language on its head, because our usual

concepts serve only to delineate a world of particulars
as seen from the perspective of an isolated and separate
ego—an individual calling itself "I." Faced with this
situation, the sage has the choice to remain silent— as
the Buddha famously did when he delivered a discourse on Truth by holding up a flower and saying
nothing—or to employ paradox to tease the intellect
out of its conventional perspective. The experience of
the enlightened may sound paradoxical, but that is
partly due to the limitations of unenlightened logic
and its language. The eye of wisdom continues to see
the play of opposites, of course, but it is no longer
blinded to the all-embracing unity that underlies, inter-
penetrates, and harmonizes them. When the conceptual veil through which we ordinarily see the world is
lifted, each limited object shines with the boundless
light of the spirit, and each transitory experience is a
celebration of eternity. As the text says, the truly wise
is one who "sees everything as nothing but the Self,
and the Self in everything he sees."

This wholeness of life, the unity-in-difference
of the manifest relative world and the unmanifest
Absolute, is known as *brahman*. It is the mysterious
holism of *brahman* that is the subject of much of
this Upanishad. That a life of the spirit is not incom-
patible with life in the world is further emphasized

by the text's use of a common device in Vedic literature, the number 100. As the inventors of the concept of zero, the ancient Indians were fascinated by
the hidden potential of "no-thing," its fecund emptiness. In the number 100 here, the two zeros sym-
bolize the fullnesses of the Absolute and relative,
and the one, their unity. Thus, when the text talks
of "aspiring to be one hundred," it means not just
enjoying a long life but living Enlightenment.

The path to the complete liberation in *brahman*
proceeds in two stages: first, a transformation into
the Divine, and then a translation of the Divine into
everything. The key to the first stage is meditation—
the settling of the mind into that silence that is its
source. Long misunderstood to be a difficult, even
ascetic undertaking, this process is in fact easy and
enjoyable. The settled state of awareness comes not
through forcibly restraining the mind but by "enjoying the inner." This refers to the mind's nature to
withdraw spontaneously from the world of change as
it entertains progressively refined levels of thinking
during meditation. The subtler levels of thinking are
increasingly charming, as they are nearer their source
in the Self, whose nature is bliss. Therefore, no effort
is needed. When all mental activity has been transcended, awareness is left by itself, pure and

unbounded. This state is initially experienced in the depths of meditation, as we have learned from the Māndūkya Upanishad. However, once the nervous system becomes purified enough, the mind is able to reflect this fundamental level of silence at all times, no matter how active it may be on the surface. The permanent awareness of the Self during all activity is the first stage of Enlightenment; it is technically known as Cosmic Consciousness.

But this is only the first part of the journey. In Cosmic Consciousness, the Self is lived as a state of radical nonattachment, a witness of everything, including the activities of the body-mind. This blissful state of subjective freedom is never over-shadowed, no matter what circumstances occur, but by comparison with the Self the objective world is a place of limited charm, a realm hedged in by restrictions and forever being eroded by transience. Thus, in Cosmic Consciousness a state of duality exists between the freedom of the Self and the limitations of the non-Self. If the highest level of evolution, the state of total Enlightenment, is to be lived, then the rift between the infinite Self and the finite world must be healed, and all of life, no matter how ephemeral, must be infused with the glory of the spirit. Full development necessitates a growth from a way of *seeing* to a way of *being with*. This proceeds through the growth of a heartfelt devotion that transforms the lucidity of unattached insight into a loving empathy with everything that arises in the theatre of experience. Cosmic Consciousness must mature into Unity Consciousness.

As it structures creation, the divine intelligence unfolds in myriad gradations of light that become increasingly less rarified, more solid. Before the transition to Unity Consciousness occurs, there is an intermediate stage known as God Consciousness when the transcendental radiance begins to be experienced on the sensory level. The scintillating innermost depth of material existence, the subtlest level of relative life becomes perceptible. In Wordsworth's phrase, "earth and every common sight" become "apparelled in celestial light."

This finest level of material creation is technically known as "the golden womb." The final four stanzas of the Īsha Upanishad address this stratum of creation in its most striking form, as the sun, the endlessly generous source of all light, life, and intelligence in our solar system. The most important of the Vedic deities, Agni, a figure who amalgamates many aspects of the divine alchemy of creation—consciousness, spirit, light, fire, and the energy of transformation—

is petitioned. These lines, recited even today at Hindu funerals, celebrate the final purification and release of karma when the limited self, for so long contracted around its ancient core of held memories, finally unravels and returns to its source in the unbounded ocean of Being.

At the heart of this phenomenal world, within
all its changing forms, dwells the unchanging
Lord.
So, go beyond the changing, and, enjoying the
inner, cease to take for your self what to others
are riches.

Continuing to act in the world, one may aspire to
be one hundred.
Thus, and only thus, can a person be free from the
binding influence of action.

Unillumined indeed are those worlds clouded by the
blinding darkness of ignorance.
Into this death sink all those whose dullness denies
the Self.

The one Self never moves, yet is too swift for the
mind.
The senses cannot reach It; It is ever beyond their
grasp.
Remaining still, It outstrips all activity, yet in It rests
the breath of all that moves.

It moves, yet moves not.
It is far, yet It is near.
It is within all this, and yet without all this.

He who sees everything as nothing but the Self, and
    the Self in everything he sees, such a seer
    withdraws from nothing.

For the enlightened, all that exists is nothing but the
    Self, so how could any suffering or delusion
    continue for those who know this Oneness?

He who pervades all is radiant, unbounded, and
    untainted.
He is the Knower, the one Mind, omnipresent and
    self-sufficient.
He has harmonized diversity throughout eternal
    time.

Into a blinding darkness go they who worship
    action alone.
Into an even greater darkness go they who worship
    meditation.

For It is other than meditation; It is other than
    action.

ĪSHA UPANISHAD

This we have heard from the enlightened ones who
teach us.

Meditation and action—he who knows these two
together, through action leaves death behind and
through meditation gains immortality.

Into a blinding darkness go they who idolize the
Absolute.
Into an even greater darkness go they who idolize
the relative.

For It is other than the relative; It is other than
the Absolute.
This we have heard from the enlightened ones who
teach us.

Absolute and relative—he who knows these two
together, through the relative leaves death
behind and through the Absolute gains
immortality.

The threshold of Reality is veiled by golden light.
Reveal It, O Lord, for the guiding purpose of my
life is to know the Truth.

O Lord of Light, the knowing one, the golden
guardian, giver of life to all, spread apart your
rays, gather up your brilliance, so I may perceive
your finest and most splendrous nature, the
cosmic spirit that lies at your heart.
For I myself am That!

Let my breath merge with the cosmic breath; may
my body be as dust.
Remember, O mind, remember what has been done.
Yes, remember, O mind, remember what has been
done!

O Agni, show us the right path, lead us to eternal
freedom, You who know everything.
May we not be diverted from our goal, for with all
devotion we submit ourselves to You.

from the Brihadāranyaka Upanishad

1

As the world is the Divine made active,
nothing in life is without significance. Each thought,
word, and deed has its consequences, producing
positive or negative effects for the actor and the
whole of creation. Because it is performed in
ignorance of this connectedness, much of human
activity is chaotic, prone to aberration and conducive
to suffering. But there does exist a class of action
that aligns us directly with the Natural Law that
organizes and governs the universe and thereby
generates the most life-supporting influences. This
activity is what we call ritual. Ritual is a means for
us human beings to play our part consciously in the
dramatic symphony of the cosmos. Ritual ennobles
even the most apparently commonplace action by
reintegrating it into its rightful sacred context.

Since the intelligence that structures each fiber
of creation is omnipresent, it can be located at any
point in time or space. The universe is thus a vast

hologram, with the potential of the totality accessible in each of its myriad fragments. These fragments are connected in a hierarchical chain of subtle correspondences, and their connections are enlivened by the science of ritual, in order to link the human to the Divine. Utilizing repetition and well-established rhythms, ritual operates through the skill of focusing highly coherent attention on a particular aspect of the microcosm in such a way as to enliven and utilize the infinite potential it contains. A crucial part of this process is the symbol. By imaging the greater in the lesser, the symbol serves to localize the abstract in the concrete and connect the microcosm to the macrocosm. Those who are schooled in the understanding of symbolism can act in conscious communion with the whole and thus bring about desired changes in the localized realm of action.

One of the most potent Vedic symbols linking the human to the cosmic was the Dawn Horse. In ancient India the kings performed a rite known as the Celebration of the Horse, in which the most magnificent white horse in the kingdom, garlanded with golden threads and with the royal seal emblazoned on its forehead, was let loose to roam free for a year. All the land it covered in this time was considered to belong by heaven's decree to the king, who, as the human embodiment of the Natural Law that governs the universe, was alone considered fit to have the majestic Dawn Horse, symbol of the universe, as his emblem. Having mapped out the sovereign's land, the horse was symbolically offered up to the gods, in fulfillment of the archetypal ritual whereby the old order is purified and renewed by being returned to its transcendent source.

Dating in its present form from around 800 B.C.E., the Brihadāranyaka ("the great forest teaching") Upanishad is the oldest of the Upanishads and also the longest, containing over four hundred sections in both verse and prose, many of them of great length and density. It is a fecund seedbed of virtually all the spiritual teachings of both the Vedic times that preceded it, and the subsequent three thousand years and more of Indian history. Four excerpts from this extraordinary body of recondite lore are included here.

OM

Truly, the head of the sacrificial horse is the dawn,
its eye the sun, its breath the wind, its open
mouth the cosmic fire.

The body of the sacrificial horse is time, its back the
heavens, its belly is space, and its hoof the
ground.

Its flanks are the four points of the compass, and its
ribs their midpoints.

Its legs are the seasons, their joints the months and
fortnights, and its feet the days and nights.

Its bones are the stars, its flesh the clouds.

The rivers are its arteries, the mountains its liver and
lungs.

The sand is its dung, and the trees and grasses its
hair.

Its front part is the sun as it rises, and its rear is the
sun as it sets.

Its shaking is the thunder, its yawning is the
lightning, its pissing is the rain, and its neighing
is sound.

Its front part, rising from the seas of the East, is the
golden day.

from the BRIHADĀRANYAKA UPANISHAD

And its rear, rising from the seas of the West, is the
silver night.

The sacrificial vessels before and behind the horse
are the two great oceans.

As a steed it bore the gods, as a stallion it bore the
celestial beings, as a hunter it bore the demons,
and as a horse it bore man.

The cosmic ocean of the Self, indeed, is its kin; the
cosmic ocean of the Self is its source.

1.I.1

At times the Upanishads employ a bewildering number of conflated metaphors and symbolic etymologies
to explain the mechanics of cosmic intelligence becoming matter. But this transformation is ultimately
an unspeakable and mysterious process of which
any description is at best only provisional, a finger
pointing at the moon. Any model is able to use only
symbols drawn from experience with which we are
familiar, and all models are inevitably reflections of
our particular level of consciousness, which, until full
Enlightenment, is unstable, evolving, and prey to dis-
tortion. This is why the Sanskrit word for a philosophical system is *darshana,* which means "a point of
view." The various descriptions of reality found in
Vedic texts are never intended to be mutually exclu-
sive, nor do they necessarily consider themselves to
be final, but they recognize that each different perspective is valid on its own level as far as it goes but
sooner or later is to be transcended.

As there is always an equivalence between the
structure of man himself and his understanding of
the structure of the universe, there is a certain logic
in depicting the Self as the Cosmic Man, whose body
is the universe. This analogy, which occurs often in

the Upanishads, is also perhaps the most apt way to depict the perspective of Unity Consciousness, in which the entire universe is recognized to be one's own Self.

The first of the following sections presents the Cosmic Man (*purusha*) as the masculine principle of inactive spirit, which manifests through the active feminine principle of matter, or Nature (*prakriti*). These two are inseparable complements of each other, and every form of their creation will bear the sign of this duality.

Any duality automatically implies a trinity: the two constituent elements and their connection. In the second section, "speech, mind, and breath" occur as an archetypal trinity of abstract principles that are then located in several other groups of three, culminating in the three great deities: Brahmā (the Boundless), his consort Saraswatī (the Pure-Flowing), and their offspring, known as Vāyu (Life Breath) or Indra, (Power). Brahmā embodies the creativity inherent in Consciousness, Saraswatī the pure knowledge that gives this creativity shape and direction. Together they engender Vāyu-Indra, the subtlest electrical energy, which, streaming forth from the Absolute, galvanizes all life.

In the beginning was the Self alone, in the form of
    Purusha, the mighty Person.
In previous times (*pūrva*) he burnt up (*ush*) all evil,
    thus he is called Purusha.
With this knowledge one devours all rivals.

Looking around, he saw no one else.
Then Purusha spoke, and his first words were:
    "I am."
Thus was I-ness born.
And even now, when a person is asked, "Who
    is it?" he replies first "It is I," and then adds
    his name.

But then Purusha became frightened—as even now
    we become frightened when alone.
He thought to himself:
"Since there is nothing but myself, what is there to
    be frightened of?"
Thereupon his fears dissolved, as he realized they
    were groundless.
For truly, fear is born of duality.

from the BRIHADĀRANYAKA UPANISHAD

But still he was not happy, for there is no happiness
    in being alone.
He wanted a companion, so he grew as large as a
    man and a woman entwined, and then divided
    himself in two, creating a husband and a wife.
(For, as Yājnyavalkya used to say, this body is but
    half of oneself, the other half is woman.)
Thus his emptiness was filled by a woman.
They came together again, and from their union
    were born all people.

But then the woman thought:
"How could he join with me when he has created
    me from himself? I must hide."
So she took the form of a cow, but he took the
    form of a bull, and joined with her again.
And from their union were born all cows.

Then she took the form of a mare, but he took the
    form of a stallion and joined with her again.
Then she took the form of a she-ass, but he took
    the form of a he-ass and joined with her again.
And from their union were born all hoofed animals.

Then she took the form of a nanny goat, but he
took the form of a billy goat and joined with
her again.
And from their union were born all goats.

Then she took the form of a ewe, but he took the
form of a ram and joined with her again.
And from their union were born all sheep.

In this way he created the male and female of all
creatures—even down to the ants.

Then he thought:
"Truly, I am the whole creation, for I have created
everything from my own Self."
Hence he is called Shrishti, the creator.

Whoever awakens to this becomes as great as
Purusha in his own creation.

1.IV.1–5

Now, Prajāpati, the lord of progeny, created for
himself the trinity of speech, mind, and breath:

Whatever sound there is is the speech of the Divine,
and all that can be expressed has its origin in
this speech.

from the BRIHADĀRANYAKA UPANISHAD

It is the mind that sees, and the mind that hears, for
we say:
"I did not see it; my mind was elsewhere; I did not
hear it; my mind was elsewhere."
Desire, imagination, doubt, faith and lack of faith,
stability and instability, shame, reasoning, and
fear—all these are just the mind.
And even if we are touched from behind, it is the
mind that notices.

The body is governed by the operation of five
breaths, but these five are all aspects of a single
breath, the breath of Life itself.

Truly, speech, mind, and breath together make up
the self.
These three are also the three worlds:
Speech is this expressed world, mind is the inner
world, and breath is the world beyond.

These three are also the Vedas:
Speech is the Rig Veda, mind is the Yajur Veda, and
breath is the Sāma Veda.

These three are also the gods, the ancestors, and
men:
Speech is the gods, mind is the ancestors, and breath
is men.

These three are also mother, father, and children:
Speech is the mother, mind is the father, and breath
is the children.

These three are what is known, what is to be
known, and what will remain unknown:
Whatever is known is a form of speech, for speech
is the expression of knowledge.
And pure knowledge is the goddess Saraswatī,
protecting all who know her.
And whatever is yet to be known is a form of mind,
for mind is to be known.
And the thought form from which the universe
arises is the god Brahmā, protecting all who
know him.
And whatever remains unknown is a form of breath,
for breath remains unknown.
And the air that presides over breath is Vāyu,
protecting all who know him.

from the BRIHADĀRANYAKA UPANISHAD

The earth is the body of Saraswatī and this fire her
shining form.
And as far as speech extends, the earth and fire
extend.
The heavens are the body of Brahmā, and the sun
his shining form.
And as far as mind extends, the sun and heavens
extend.

Brahmā and Saraswatī came together and from their
union Vāyu was born.
Vāyu is Indra, the ruler of heaven, unrivaled—for
rivalry comes only from a second.
Whoever understands the meaning of this has no rival.

Water is the body of Vāyu, and his shining form is
the moon.
And as far as breath extends, the waters and moon
extend.

All these threes are equal and eternal.
Whoever worships them as finite entities wins only
a finite world, but whoever worships them as
infinite attains infinity itself.

1.V.3–13

The mighty King Janaka ruled over the kingdom
of Videha from his sophisticated capital Mithilā.
As the father of Lord Rāma's wife, Sītā, heroine
of the Rāmāyana, Janaka is cherished as an ideal
because he was not only a wise and able ruler but
also a great seeker after Truth. Indeed, so great
was his desire for Enlightenment that at one point
he was prepared to renounce his entire kingdom
for the gift of sacred knowledge.

Janaka's life as the embodiment of both material
and spiritual fullness demonstrates that even the
most exalted material circumstances stand in need
of spirituality. But on the other hand, there is no
necessary connection between a person's social
position and his level of consciousness. Someone
may live in a cave as a recluse and still cling to
worldly desires, while another person may live
in a palace yet be unattached to material things.
What is important is not the outer situation but
the inner state. Whatever our position in life, the
important thing is that the mind should begin to
transcend the outer environment and contact its
source in transcendental consciousness. It is this

expansion of awareness, rather than any particular
way of life, that is the true starting point of the
spiritual life.

The great sage Yājnyavalkya is one of the most
endearing characters in the early texts, displaying
intellectual agility, a wicked sense of humor, and
a refreshing freedom from religiosity. Though the
charm of the puns and wordplay so prevalent in
the original Sanskrit is lost in translation, the
following passages at least give an idea of the
playfulness that often lightens even the most
serious of his philosophical debates. While
many of these discuss at length the nested and
hierarchical categories of existence that make up
life, Yājnyavalkya's ultimate aim is always to expose
the transcendental unity that underlies all diversity.
To this end, the Master will gently, even mischie-
vously, lead his students out of their habitual
thought patterns to the direct experience of Reality
itself. Through the progressive deconstruction
of their conceptual frameworks, his pupils have
eventually to surrender their desire to reduce
reality to an intellectual model. Even the ultimate
philosophical questions about birth, death, and
meaning must be surrendered, for the play of life

is without beginning or end; it is a glorious
mystery that thought alone can never solve.
This seems to bc the message of Yājnyavalkya's
parting riddle.

Janaka, the king of Videha, had a sacrifice performed
at which many gifts were distributed to the officiat-
ing priests. A great number of brahmins from the
lands of Kuru and Pānchāla were gathered there for
the occasion.

Now, it happened that the king wished to find
out which of these wise men was the most learned in
Vedic lore. So he had a thousand cows put in a pen,
and from the horns of each cow were hung ten
gold coins. "Venerable brahmins," he announced,
"whichever of you is the most learned may take these
cows home with him." But not one of the brahmins
dared step forward. Then the sage Yājnyavalkya
turned to his favorite pupil Sāmashravas and said,
"Drive these cows home for me, my dear." So
Sāmashravas drove them away. The assembled brahmins were furious: "How dare he call himself the
most learned among us!" And each of them resolved
to test Yājnyavalkya on his knowledge.

3.I.1–2

Ashvala, the specialist in making offerings, asked
how those who perform the sacrifices obtain

freedom and examined him on the details of the sacrificial chants and oblations, the divinities and the hymns of praise. Ārtabhāga, from the Jāratkārus, questioned him on the senses and their objects, and then on the nature of death. Bhujyu, grandson of Lāhyā, asked him about the fate of those who perform the horse sacrifice. And then Ushasta, son of Chakra, and Kahola, son of Kaushītakī, questioned him on the nature of *brahman,* the Self of all beings. After he had answered each of these questions satisfactorily, Gārgī, the daughter of Vāchaknu, stepped forward:

"Yājnyavalkya," she asked, "If this whole world is woven warp and weft from water, from what is water woven, warp and weft?"

"It is woven from air, O Gārgī."

"Then from what is air woven, warp and weft?"

"From the heavens, O Gārgī."

"Then from what are the heavens woven, warp and weft?"

"From the realms of celestial sound, O Gārgī."

"Then from what are the realms of celestial sound woven, warp and weft?"

"From the realms of the sun, O Gārgī."

"Then from what are the realms of the sun woven, warp and weft?"

"From the realms of the moon, O Gārgī."

"Then from what are the realms of the moon woven, warp and weft?"

"From the realms of the stars, O Gārgī."

"Then from what are the realms of the stars woven, warp and weft?"

"From the realms of the gods, O Gārgī."

"Then from what are the realms of the gods woven, warp and weft?"

"From the realm of Indra, the king of gods, O Gārgī."

"Then from what is the realm of Indra woven, warp and weft?"

"From the realm of Prajāpati, the father of all, O Gārgī."

"Then from what is the realm of Prajāpati woven, warp and weft?"

"From the realm of Brahmā, the Creator, O Gārgī."

"Then from what is the realm of Brahmā, the Creator, woven, warp and weft?"

"O Gārgī," replied Yājnyavalkya, "do not ask so many questions, lest your head fall off. You are asking too much about that divinity of whom we should not ask."

Thereupon Gārgī stepped down and held her peace.

3.VI.1

Then Uddālaka, son of Āruna, came forward and questioned him on the many different worlds and their relationships, and on the Self, their inner essence. After Yājnyavalkya had satisfied Uddālaka in full, Gārgī returned to question him again. This time she asked him about the nature of space, and then about the Imperishable itself. Following her, Vidagdhah, from the family of Shakalya, approached him, asking:

"How many divine beings are there, Yājnyavalkya?"

Yājnyavalkya replied by quoting the Rig Veda·

"As many as are mentioned in the Nivid, the hymn to all the gods; that is, three hundred and three, and three thousand and three."

"Yes, Yājnyavalkya, but how many divine beings are there really?"

"Thirty-three."

"Yes, Yājnyavalkya, but how many divine beings are there really?"

"Six."

"Yes, Yājnyavalkya, but how many divine beings are there really?"

"Three."

"Yes, Yājnyavalkya, but how many divine beings are there really?"

"Two."

"Yes, Yājnyavalkya, but how many divine beings are there really?"

"One and a half."

"Yes, Yājnyavalkya, but how many divine beings are there really?"

"One!"

"Very well, Yājnyavalkya, now tell me who those three hundred and three, and three thousand and three divine beings are."

"In fact," Yājnyavalkya replied, "there are just thirty-three divine beings. All the others are but different forms of these thirty-three."

"And who are these thirty-three?"

"They are the eight Vasus, the eleven Rudras, the twelve Ādityas—that makes thirty-one. And Indra and Prajāpati make thirty-three."

"And who are the eight Vasus?"

"Agni, the fire, and his consort Prithivī, the earth. Vāyu, the wind, and his consort Antariksha, the sky. Āditya, the sun, and his consort Dyau, the heavens. Chandramas, the moon, and Nakshatra, the stars. Among all these does this world dwell (*vās*); hence they are called the Vasus."

"And who are the eleven Rudras?"

"They are the intelligences operating in the five organs of sense, and the intelligences operating in the five organs of action. These make ten, and the individual soul is the eleventh. When they depart from this mortal body they make us weep (*rud*); hence they are called the Rudras."

"And who are the twelve Ādityas?"

"They are the twelve months of the year, the spokes of the wheel of time. And as they turn they carry the whole world along (*ādā*); hence they are called the Ādityas."

"And who is Indra, and who is Prajāpati?"

"Indra is the thunder, and Prajāpati the sacrifice."

"And what is the essence of thunder?"

"The thunderbolt."

from the BRIHADĀRANYAKA UPANISHAD

"And what is the essence of the sacrifice?"
    "The offerings."

"Now, Yājnyavalkya, who are those six divine beings?"
    "The cosmic fire, the earth, the wind, the sky, the sun, and the heavens. These are the six—the whole world is made from them."

"Then tell me who the three divine beings are."
    "The three worlds: earth, which is body; space, which is breath; and the heavens, which are mind. Within them all these other divine beings have their life."

"And who are the two divine beings?"
    "Matter and Life."

"And who are the one and a half divine beings?"
    "He who purifies."
    But then the assembled priests objected, saying: "He who purifies is one. How then can he be called one and a half (*adhyārdha*)?"
    To which Yājnyavalkya replied, "It is because of him that this whole world evolved (*adhyārdhnot*); hence he is called Adhyārdha."

"And who then is the one divine being?"

"The very breath of life, what they call *brahman,* or THAT."

3.1X.1–9

When Shakalya had at last finished, Yājnyavalkya turned to the assembled brahmins and said: "O venerable brahmins, if any one of you wishes to question me further, you may do so, or all of you together may question me. Or I will question any one of you who wishes me to, or I will question all of you together."

But not one of the brahmins dared accept his challenge. Thus was Yājnyavalkya proved the wisest among them. But before he departed, Yājnyavalkya gave them this riddle: "Man is like a mighty tree; his hair the leaves, his skin the bark. Blood flows through his skin as sap flows through the bark, for a wounded man bleeds blood as an injured tree seeps sap. His flesh is like the inner bark, his nerves its fibrous threads; his bones are like the wood within, his marrow as the pith. A tree when felled sprouts again from the root, but from what root is man reborn when he's cut down by death? Do not say from the semen, for that comes from the living—as saplings spring from seeds of trees that have not died.

from the BRIHADĀRANYAKA UPANISHAD

A tree will sprout anew so long as its roots remain,
but from what root is man reborn when he's cut
down by death?

"Well, once born, he's never really born again,
for who could recreate him? *Brahman* is knowledge!
Brahman is bliss! *Brahman* is the only goal—both of
those who make offerings, and those who still the
mind and know."

3.IX.28

Desire is usually held to be the main obstacle on
the road to Enlightenment, and many systems have
advocated its forcible suppression as indispensable
to liberation. The Upanishads generally exhibit
a more generous and life-affirming attitude toward
this thorny question. They see desire as the universal driving force behind all evolution. It was the
Divine's desire for the joy of variety that caused
It to create the world, and it is the creative urging
of desire that has impelled all life ever since. Thus,
to the wise, desire is a natural phenomenon,
embedded in the very tissue of existence. As desire
is born from a sense of lack (the original meaning
of our word "want"), it is always a desire for more—
more love, more happiness, more power, more
knowledge. This desire for more is ingrained in us
all, propelling our life from the moment we first
blindly reach for our mother's breast. Even the
most altruistic action is performed because it gives
the performer more joy; even the monk, it can be
argued, has sublimated all his worldly desires into
one grand spiritual desire: the desire for God.
So although many religious systems have tried to

control desire, they have not brought widespread happiness. In the end all such attempts must fail, for they are as futile as trying to legislate against the sap rising anew each spring.

And yet, as we all experience, the realization of our desires does not bring us permanent happiness. Desire breeds desire, and even when we have more than enough, we seem relentlessly driven to accumulate yet more in a society whose economic future is believed to depend on continually increasing material consumption of an ever more frenetic and destructive sort. Sometimes it even seems that it is not really the attainment of a desired object or experience that we are seeking, but a return to the state of equilibrium that existed before that particular desire arose.

We are caught in the barbed net of desires because they are generally directed only outward toward the world; desire is born from the gap between self and other and always seeks to close this gap. The Upanishads recognize that, like Shake-speare's Cleopatra, we have "immortal longings" but teach that it is possible to remove one thorn by using another. If we can utilize the dynamic of desire in an inward direction, it will provide the momentum

to transport the mind and heart to what is really
the goal of all desiring: the Self. For although we
do not realize it, only the immortal Self can provide
that permanent contentment that we all crave, only
the Self can give us the nourishment, happiness,
and fulfilment we vainly spend our lives seeking in
the world of things around us. So the desire for anything is, ultimately, the desire for the Divine. This is
why desire is so persistent, so implacable. Seen in
this light, desire is an ally, not an enemy, serving the
purpose of evolution by expanding the little self,
which always suffers lack, in the direction of the
Self, the source and goal of all.

　　To employ the natural desire for more in an
inward direction is the art of meditation. It is the
gratifying nature of the subtler levels of thinking
that draw the mind naturally to settle down toward
its source. The Upanishads do not, of course, advo-
cate the unbridled gratification of all desire, but its
gradual refinement. This comes about quite naturally,
as the more the Self is contacted in meditation,
the more It seeps into the very nature of the mind,
bestowing an abiding sense of satisfaction and
happiness. Outwardly directed desires spontaneously
become less binding, more life-supporting for the

individual and the whole environment because they are not driven by the neurotic craving that comes from a sense of inner emptiness aching to be filled. And the more Self-realization develops, the more all worldly satisfactions begin to be appreciated as but a pale reflection of the bliss of Enlightenment.

Now Yājnyavalkya had two wives, Maitreyī and Katyāyanī. Maitreyī loved to discuss Enlightenment, while Katyāyanī was more interested in domestic things. When the time had come to renounce the ways of a householder and become a recluse in the forest, Yājnyavalkya called Maitreyī and said to her: "It is time for me to give up this worldly life, so let me make a final settlement with you and Katyāyanī."

But Maitreyī replied: "Even if the whole world and all its wealth were mine, would that bring me immortality?"

"No," said Yājnyavalkya, "your life would be as that of any other who had many riches. But such wealth will never buy you immortality."

"So what is the use of having something that will not bring me immortality?" replied Maitreyī. "Give me instead, my lord, the benefit of your knowledge."

"You have always been dear to me, Maitreyī, but now through asking this, you have become even more dear. I shall teach you, my beloved, but listen very carefully to what I say:

"Truly, it is not for the sake of the husband that the husband is dear, but for the sake of the Self. And it is not for the sake of the wife that the wife is dear, but for the sake of the Self. And it is not for the sake of the sons that the sons are dear, but for the sake of the Self. And it is not for the sake of wealth that wealth is dear, but for the sake of the Self. And it is not for the sake of cattle that cattle are dear, but for the sake of the Self. And it is not for the sake of the priest that the priest is dear, but for the sake of the Self. And it is not for the sake of the gods that the gods are dear, but for the sake of the Self. And it is not for the sake of the Vedas that the Vedas are dear, but for the sake of the Self. And it is not for the sake of the many beings that the many beings are dear, but for the sake of the Self. And it is not for the sake of the All that the All is dear, but for the sake of the Self.

"Indeed, my beloved, it is the Self that should be seen, the Self that should be heard, the Self that should be reflected upon, and the Self that should be known. And when the Self has been seen, when the Self has been heard, when the Self has been reflected upon, and when the Self has been known, then everything is known."

4.V.1–6

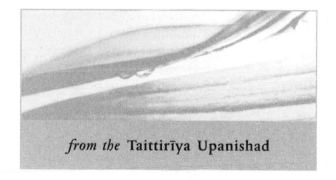

from the Taittirīya Upanishad

THE ROOT TEACHING of the Upanishads is that life is bliss. Specifically, *brahman* is traditionally described as *sat-chit-ānanda*. *Sat* means eternal and unchanging Being; because Being has the self-referring quality of intelligence, it is also *chit:* Consciousness. And this state of unbounded freedom is by its nature *ānanda:* bliss. It is by bliss that the multifarious levels of the universal order are held in harmony and balance, and it is the expansion of bliss that is the purpose of creation.

On the human level, bliss is not mere pleasure; it transcends all that the senses can provide, individually or collectively. Nor is it just an intensified form of what we know as happiness. Our usual happiness is a mood derived from some circumstance or experience, and, being contingent, can easily lurch into its opposite—unhappiness—when circumstances change. But the bliss the Upanishads celebrate is more than just feeling good in the waking state; it is a joy that depends on nothing other than itself. Uncaused, it is the ecstasy intrinsic in just being fully conscious. Certainly, such bliss may be magnified by events in the outside world, as the ocean is given form by its waves, but in itself it is unshakable and self-sufficient because it is the very source and ground of everything that arises. As the hidden nature of life, bliss is as eternal and unending as life itself. And like life, it has no opposite.

Brahman is said to be a mass of unimaginably concentrated bliss, and it is our conscious contact with *brahman* that is blissful. The possibility of this contact draws the mind effortlessly inward during meditation; it occurs when the individual awareness transcends all sense of separation and expands to become the Self.

This teaching does not overlook the fact that for most of us life is anything but blissful. According to the sages, we do not generally experience life as bliss because we have acted out of harmony with Natural Law, the will of God, and therefore we do not enjoy the world aright. What we call suffering is a necessary karmic consequence of our aberrant behavior, a slap administered by Mother Nature to wake us up and put us back on the right path. The greater the deviation, the harder the slap. But however difficult our circumstances may appear, from the expanded point of view of those who have arrived, embodied human existence is the irreversible journey—albeit lengthy, circuitous, and often testing—to an ever greater and more authentic familiarity with bliss. Seen from the mountaintop, we are dolls made of salt on our way to the sea.

The sages of the Upanishads always remind us that their wisdom has no human genesis but is the natural expression of the organizing power inherent in the very nature of universal Consciousness itself. In the second half of the passage below, cosmic intelligence is personified by Varuna, lord of the waters (who was to become Ahura Mazda, supreme deity of the Zoroastrians in ancient Persia). As ruler of the invisible worlds, he presides over the relationship of mankind and the gods; here he passes on the knowledge of *brahman* to Brighu ("Crackling of the ritual fire"), the father of one of the most important families of Vedic seers.

In the beginning this universe was not.
There was just pure potential, from which was then
    born Being.
And from Being was born the Self, which is known
    as perfect.

Truly, that perfect Self is the essence of existence.
Truly, in tasting the essence one rejoices in bliss.
Indeed, who could breathe, who could live, were
    there not this all-pervading bliss?
Truly, it is this essence that bestows bliss.

Truly, when a person discovers a foundation of
    fearlessness in the Self, in that which is invisible,
    formless, unlimited, and self-sufficient, then has
    he found true fearlessness.
If, however, he makes in this unity even the smallest
    gap, then fear is born.
To all whose self is small, the form of the formless
    brings fear.

Because of this, it is said:

from the TAITTIRĪYA UPANISHAD

From fear of Him the wind blows, from fear of Him
the sun rises, from fear of Him the cosmic fire
and cosmic waters move, and from fear of Him
death hurries on.

Now follows the teaching concerning bliss:
Imagine a young person: pure, quick, well-read,
resolute, healthy, and having all the wealth of
the world.
Let this be one unit of human bliss.

One hundred times greater than this human bliss is
the bliss of the lower celestial musicians—and
no less is the bliss of one who is learned in the
Vedas and not consumed by desire.
One hundred times greater than the bliss of the
lower celestial musicians is the bliss of the
higher celestial musicians—and no less is the
bliss of one who is learned in the Vedas and not
consumed by desire.
One hundred times greater than the bliss of the
higher celestial musicians is the bliss of the
ancestors in Paradise—and no less is the bliss
of one who is learned in the Vedas and not
consumed by desire.

One hundred times greater than the bliss of the ancestors in Paradise is the bliss of the gods who were born divine—and no less is the bliss of one who is learned in the Vedas and not consumed by desire.

One hundred times greater than the bliss of the gods who were born divine is the bliss of the gods who gained their divinity through good deeds—and no less is the bliss of one who is learned in the Vedas and not consumed by desire.

One hundred times greater than the bliss of the gods who gained their divinity through good deeds is the bliss of the higher gods—and no less is the bliss of one who is learned in the Vedas and not consumed by desire.

One hundred times greater than the bliss of the higher gods is the bliss of Indra, king of the gods—and no less is the bliss of one who is learned in the Vedas and not consumed by desire.

One hundred times greater than the bliss of Indra, king of the gods, is the bliss of Brihaspati, teacher of the gods—and no less is the bliss of one who is learned in the Vedas and not consumed by desire.

from the TAITTIRĪYA UPANISHAD

One hundred times greater than the bliss of
Brihaspati, teacher of the gods, is the bliss of
Prajāpati, father of all—and no less is the bliss
of one who is learned in the Vedas and not
consumed by desire.

One hundred times greater than the bliss of
Prajāpati, father of all, is the bliss of Brahmā, the
Creator—and no less is the bliss of one who is
learned in the Vedas and not consumed by
desire.

The Self that is here in a person, and the Self that is
there in the sun, He is one.

Whoever knows this, on leaving the world behind,
passes through the self made of matter, through
the self made of life energy, through the self
made of mind, through the self made of
knowledge, and reaches the self made of bliss.

There is more to hear of this:

That from which words turn back and the mind
cannot grasp, that is It.

He who enjoys the bliss of *brahman* has no fear
whatsoever.

He is not worried by the thoughts:

"Why did I not do what is right? Why did I do
what is wrong?"
He who knows *brahman* escapes from the clutches of
both.
Thus is the Upanishad.

Bhrigu, the scintillating one, approached his father,
Varuna, lord of the waters, and said: "Sir, teach
me about *brahman.*"
Varuna taught him of matter, life, sight, hearing,
mind, and speech.

Then he added: "Seek to know that from which
all these are born, by which they are sustained,
and into which they return."
Bhrigu retired and meditated, and through
meditation he saw that matter is *brahman.*
For, indeed, from matter all beings are born, by
matter they are sustained, and into matter
they again return.

Having realized this, he again approached his
father and said: "Noble sir, teach me of
brahman."
Varuna replied: "Seek to know *brahman* through
meditation, for *brahman* is meditation."

from the TAITTIRĪYA UPANISHAD

Bhrigu retired and meditated, and through
   meditation he saw that life is *brahman.*
For, indeed, from life all beings are born, by life
   they are sustained, and into life they again
   return.

Having realized this, he again approached his father
   and said: "Honored sir, teach me of *brahman.*"
Varuna replied: "Seek to know *brahman* through
   meditation, for *brahman* is meditation."
Bhrigu retired and meditated, and through
   meditation he saw that mind is *brahman.*
For, indeed, from mind all beings are born, by mind
   they are sustained, and into mind they again
   return.

Having realized this, he again approached his father
   and said: "Venerable sir, teach me of *brahman.*"
Varuna replied: "Seek to know *brahman* through
   meditation, for *brahman* is meditation."
Bhrigu retired and meditated, and through
   meditation he saw that intelligence is *brahman.*
For, indeed, from intelligence all beings are born,
   by intelligence they are sustained, and into
   intelligence they again return.

Having realized this, he again approached his father and said: "Revered sir, teach me of *brahman*."

Varuna replied: "Seek to know *brahman* through meditation, for *brahman* is meditation."

Bhrigu retired and meditated, and through meditation he realized that *brahman* is bliss.

For, truly, from bliss all beings are born, by bliss they are sustained, and into bliss they again return.

This wisdom that Varuna taught Bhrigu is the Highest.

He who knows it becomes established in the Highest.

He becomes the possessor and enjoyer of riches, great in fame, great in offspring, great in cattle, and great in the splendour of sacred wisdom.

2.VII.1–3.VI.1

Mundaka Upanishad

WHEN VIEWED in the light of the Divine, life is a sacred drama that takes the form of a continuous ritual of sacrifice. The supreme instance of this is the primordial self-sacrifice whereby the Cosmic Man, symbolizing the Absolute, gives birth to the world of multiplicity by dividing his body into myriad parts. This original offering is constantly reenacted at every level of life. And as an intrinsic part of this process, our existence as an individual is likewise a perpetual transformation of energies— physical, sexual, social, emotional, financial, psychic, spiritual. We cannot escape taking part in this sacrifice, as instigator, instrument, and victim. What is vital is that we participate in the process consciously and correctly. The voluntary assumption of our born duty to align ourselves with the law of sacrifice allows us to find our rightful place in the universal order, derive legitimate benefit from it, and play our destined part in its maintenance.

As a means to this end, the central ritual around which Vedic society organized itself was the fire sacrifice (*yajnya*), in which offerings are made into the sacred fire accompanied by recitation of Sanskrit mantras specifically chosen to stimulate positive influences in nature and pacify accumulated negativity. Just as the information revolution has exploited the subtle electromagnetic field, bridging huge distances in time and space to bring us various benefits, so the *yajnya* utilizes an even deeper field: the causal level from which life is administered. This area is governed by a hierarchy of subtle intelligences known as *devas* ("the shining ones"), discarnate energies regulating the laws of nature that conduct the evolutionary process. Personified as the numerous divine beings of Vedic mythology, these complementary and varied energies are the various impulses of the one absolute causal energy. The purpose of the fire sacrifice is to gain the support of these powers.

Whereas much Vedic literature deals with the mechanics of the innumerable levels of existence, and with humanity's connection and communication with the higher beings in the different strata of creation, the Upanishads are more concerned with the Absolute from which all existence comes. As such, they are a distillation of the Vedic wisdom. But the Mundaka Upanishad takes this refinement one stage further. While remaining at the heart of orthodox tradition, it presents a radical critique of the very foundations on which the complex superstructure of sacerdotal knowledge rests. Going beyond the consolations offered by conventional religion, it presents a "higher knowledge" whereby the very problem of experiencing oneself as an isolated individual in need of salvation is itself transcended. While recognizing there will always be those individuals who need the solace of conventional religion, and those situations that require the intervention of correctly practiced sacred ritual, this revolutionary text teaches that ultimate liberation lies not in the self-fulfillment offered by the promise of worldly advancement or imagined spiritual security but in total self-transcendence. From this point of view, any attempt to bolster or continue the separate sense of self, whether in this life or in some pleasurable realm hereafter, is to remain stuck in the isolated sense of "I" that is the root cause of all our suffering in the first place. So sacrifice—from the Latin *sacer facere,* "to make sacred"—now becomes not only a priestly ritual but, at a higher level, the mind's total letting go of everything it has known, expected, or feared to allow it to gain its infinite status as the Self. This is the most valuable offering, given into the flames of transformation that consume ignorance, attachment, and suffering. Only this

unstinting surrender can unclench the closed fist
of egotism and release the chronically contracted
sense of self that is our normal reality.

In truth, everything arises in order to disappear;
everything we have, everything we think we are,
must at some point be surrendered, for it is only on
loan from the bounty of the Divine. This is how evolution proceeds, changing one state into the next,
from moment to moment, life to life. To continue in
harmony with this cosmic process, we must realize
that we surrender in order to gain. The internalizing
of the universal law of sacrifice is the meaning
behind the biblical phrase: "They that lose their life
shall find it."

The creative tension between religious forms,
which are always tending to stagnate, and the well-
spring of direct spiritual experience is a recurring
energizer in all cultures. In post-Vedic India it
inspired many waves of religious and social reform.
In the sixth century B.C.E., at a time when the Vedic
teaching was in decline, the Buddha taught a return
to first principles by rejecting empty belief and
ineffective ritual and advocating the purification of
the mind through meditation. Some four hundred
years later, the core of the most popular Hindu
scripture, the *Bhagavad Gītā,* is the passage (2.45)

114 where Lord Krishna, embodiment of the Divine, gives the same advice to Arjuna, the warrior-hero who personifies the human predicament. Such revivals have taken place many times, but it is here in the Mundaka Upanishad that the radically self-transcending nature of Vedic teaching is first and most boldly spelled out.

Brahmā, "the Boundless," is first-born among the
gods.
He is the creator of everything; remaining hidden,
he sustains all he has made.
It was he who revealed the knowledge of *brahman,*
the knowledge of that which is beyond birth,
the knowledge which is the foundation of all
other knowledge, to the seer Atharva.

Atharva taught it to Angir, the brilliant one.
Angir passed it on to Satyvāha, son of Bhāradvāja,
the swift one.
And Satyavāha, the conveyor of truth, taught both
the lower and higher knowledge to Angiras, the
fiery, in turn.

There was once a renowned man of the world
named Shaunaka.
With customary reverence he approached Angiras
and asked:
"Sir, what is that knowledge which is the key to
knowing everything?"

"Those who know *brahman*," Angiras replied,
"say that there are two kinds of knowledge—
the higher and the lower.

The lower is that of the four Vedas—Rik, Sāma,
Yajus, and Atharva, and of their accompanying
sciences: pronunciation, ritual, grammar,
etymology, meter, and knowledge of the
heavens.

The higher is that through which the Eternal
is directly experienced.
That which cannot be seen and is beyond thought,
which is without cause or parts, which neither
perceives nor acts, which is unchanging,
all-pervading, omnipresent, subtler than the
subtlest, that is the Eternal that the wise know
to be the source of all.

Just as a spider spins forth its thread and draws it in
again, the whole creation is woven from *brahman*
and unto It returns.
Just as plants are rooted in the earth, all beings are
supported by *brahman*.
Just as hair grows from a person's head, so does
everything arise from *brahman*.

From its own meditation *brahman* expands.
From this comes the life force.
From the life force universal Mind evolves.
Mind gives birth to the essential elements, and
    from these the many worlds and all their planes
    take form.
These worlds are the realms of action.
And through action comes the chance of immortality.

From *brahman,* the all-seeing, the all-knowing, whose
    meditation is infinite wisdom, from this silent
    womb is born the Creator, Brahmā, he who molds
    the swelling life force into matter, name, and
    form.

This is the truth of the lower and the higher:

The rituals, seen by the seers as the sacred verses,
    are variously explained in the three Vedas.
Perform them constantly, you who desire truth, for
    they are your path to the world of the good.
When the sacred fire is kindled, and the flame is
    rising, place your offering here with devotion
    between the holy vessels.

But if the sacrifice of fire is not followed by that of
the new moon, and the full moon sacrifice is not
followed by that of the four months and that
of the harvest; and if guests are not invited, if
offerings are not given, or given wrongly, if the
gods are not invoked—if any of these conditions
are not met, the seven worlds stay closed.

The flame has seven licking tongues: Kālī, the dark
one; the terrible; the swift-as-thought; the
crimson one; the smoky-colored; the sparkling
one; and Devī, she who takes all forms.

Whoever performs the sacrifice correctly, when these
seven are enlivened, he is led by them, as the
rays of the sun, to the world of the lord of
the gods.

The radiant ones invite him: 'Come! Come!' carrying
him up on the rays of the sun.
They honor and glorify him, saying: 'This is the
holy world of Brahmā, won by all your rituals.'

But verily, these rituals are unsafe boats; they cannot
reach the farthest shore.
The Vedic sciences are but the lower knowledge.

The ignorant, who take them as the higher, sink
    once more into old age and death.

Though they think themselves wise and learned,
    they are fools lost in ignorance, a prey to
    suffering, wandering without direction, like the
    blind led by the blind.

These ignorant children, bound by duality, think
    their journey has ended.
Blinded by attachment, they fail to see the Truth.

These deluded souls, taking rituals and merit to be
    supreme, know nothing of what is higher.
Even though they have won enjoyment in the most
    exalted heaven, they must come back again to
    this world, or even go to a lower one.

But those who live in the forest, faithfully following
    a life of meditation, they are the knowers,
    tranquil, living on charity.
Free from attachment, they leave the body through
    the gate of the sun, and reach the supreme Self,
    the imperishable spirit.

Looking on those worlds won by ritual, a true
brahmin arrives at dispassion.
For that which is not made comes not through what
is done.

For the gift of this knowledge approach a master,
one both learned in the scriptures and
established in *brahman.*
To him who has properly approached, kindling in
hand, whose mind is calm and quiet, let the
teacher impart in its fullness the knowledge of
brahman, that which leads to the imperishable
spirit, the Truth.

This is the Truth:

Thousands of sparks leap from a blazing fire, yet
each separate and individual spark remains in
essence one with the fire.
Just so, my friend, all beings arise from the
imperishable Purusha, and in time return
to It.

Purusha is the shining yet formless cosmic spirit,
the Self of the Universe.

He is within everything and without everything,
   unborn, untainted by either breath or mind.
He is beyond even the tendency to take form.

Yet from Him are born breath, mind, and the
   senses, and in their turn space, air, fire,
   water, and lastly earth, the foundation
   of all.

Light is His head, the sun and moon His eyes, space
   His ears, the Vedas His voice, the wind His
   breath, the whole world His heart, and the
   ground His feet.
Truly He is the innermost essence of all that exists.

From Him comes energy, whose burning is the sun.
From this comes Soma, and from the Soma rain.
And from this come the plants and food.
Nourished by them, the male pours seed into the
   female.
Thus the whole multitude of beings come ultimately
   from Him.

From Him arise all hymns and chants, all rituals
   and initiations, all ceremonies and offerings, the

sacred calendar and priesthood, and the various
worlds of the afterlife.
From Him are born the many deities.
From Him are born the angelic beings, and man,
and the beasts and birds, and the rice and corn,
even the very air we breathe.
From Him come meditation, stability, purity, order,
and Truth.

From Him have sprung the seven gates of sense:
the eyes, the ears, the nostrils, and the mouth;
the seven senses' spheres; the seven sense
perceptions; the seven kinds of knowledge
stemming from the senses, and the seven subtle
centers shining in the body.

From Him arise the mountains and the seas.
From Him spring rivers of every kind.
And from Him have come the herbs and juices that
sustain our very being.

Purusha is truly the whole universe, the immortal
source of all creation, all action, all meditation.
Whoever discovers Him, hidden deep within, cuts
through the bonds of ignorance—even during
his life on earth.

At the core of all stirs the hidden pulse of *brahman*.
It is the heart of everything—all that moves or
    breathes or blinks.
That which is both the eternal and the time-bound,
    the goal of all desiring, beyond all
    understanding, know That, my friend, to be the
    quintessence of life.

That which is shining, subtler than the subtlest, in
    which the many worlds and their inhabitants have
    their being, that is the imperishable *brahman*.
It is life, It is speech, It is mind.
It is the Real, It is immortality.
It, above all, you should know.
So, dear Shaunaka, know It.

Taking the great weapon of the Upanishad as your
    bow, place upon it the arrow of the mind, made
    pure and sharp by meditation.
Draw it back with a will made strong by
    contemplation of the Eternal.
Then, my friend, release the mind, let it fly from the
    bow, and swiftly find its target.

Meditate with the mantra as your bow, awareness
    the arrow, and *brahman* still the target.
Free from the distractions of the senses, take aim,
    release the mind, let it fly to *brahman,* and
    become one with It as the arrow becomes one
    with the target.

That, from whom heaven and earth and the sky
    between are woven, the loom of mind and
    senses, know It, alone, to be the Self.
Leave behind all vain words and idle thinking,
    for this is the bridge to immortality.

The subtle energies of the body spread out like
    spokes from a hub, and where they meet, there is
    found the all-supporting *brahman*.
Realize the Self as OM.
Thus may you safely cross the waters of darkness
    and reach the farther shore of light.

The Self is all-knowing, It is all-understanding, and
    to It belongs all glory.
It is pure consciousness, dwelling in the heart of all,
    in the divine citadel of Brahmā.
There is no space It does not fill.

Dwelling deep within, It manifests as mind, which
    silently directs both body and senses.
The wise behold this Self, blissful and immortal,
    shining forth through everything.

When It is seen to be both the higher and the
    lower, all doubts and uncertainties dissolve.
The knot of the heart is loosed.
One is no longer bound to action or its fruits.

The golden realms of the celestial are the subtlest
    levels of life.
Within them lies *brahman*.
Pure, indivisible, brilliant, It is the light of lights.
They who know the Self know this.

It is not lit by the light of the sun, nor by the light
    of the moon, nor by stars, nor by lightning, and
    certainly not by fire.
Only through Its light do all these others shine.
It is the light of the world, and by Its shining all
    is seen.

Brahman is immortal.

It stretches before and behind, to the left and to the
right, above and below.
It truly is the whole universe.
It is supreme.

Two birds, inseparable companions, perch on the
same tree.
One eats the fruit, while the other just looks on.

The first bird is our individual self, feeding on the
pleasures and pains of this world; the other is
the universal Self, silently witnessing all.

The individual self, immersed in the world of
change, is deluded and laments its lack of
freedom.
But when it discovers the Lord, full of dignity and
power, it is freed from all its suffering.

So, when you meet the golden Lord, the creator, the
universal spirit, the source of Brahmā himself,
then, knowing the highest, untainted by good or
evil, you will have reached the supreme.

Truly, *brahman* is life itself, shining through all
    beings.
Knowing It, the wise can talk of nothing else.
And he who, swimming in the bliss of the Self,
    delighting in its play, still enjoys a life of action,
    he is the greatest of those who know *brahman*.

When the mind and body have been purified
    through meditation, through Truth, through
    understanding and simplicity, then the perfected
    ones behold the Self, pure and brilliant.

The unchanging prevails, not the changing.
The unchanging alone brings lasting fulfillment.
The unchanging knowledge is the divine path that
    takes the wise to Truth.

Beyond all conception, the universal light shines
    forth.
It is the great One, smaller than the smallest, farther
    than the farthest, nearer than the nearest.
The wise know It resting deep within.

The eyes cannot see It, speech cannot describe It,
    nor any sense perceive It.

MUNDAKA UPANISHAD

It is not attained by effort, nor through austerities.
Only when meditation has purified the mind can
　　you know the One beyond all divisions.

The mind is kept ever active by the senses.
When they have withdrawn and the mind becomes
　　still, then the subtle Self shines forth.

When the mind rests steady and pure, then whatever
　　you desire, those desires are fulfilled, and
　　whatever you think of, those thoughts
　　materialize.
So, you who desire good fortune, revere the knower
　　of the Self.
For he who knows the Self knows the supreme
　　abode of *brahman,* in which the whole universe
　　lies resplendent.

The wise, free from all desire, devoted to this cosmic
　　spirit, cast off all attachment.

You who remain attached to action are bound by
　　your desires and must be reborn continually—
　　both during life and after death.
But when you find the Self, the goal of all desiring,
　　you will leave both birth and death behind.

This Self cannot be realized by studying the
  scriptures, nor through the use of reason, nor
  from the words of others—no matter what
  they say.
By the grace of the Self the Self is known; the Self
  reveals Itself.

It cannot be attained by the weak, nor by the
  halfhearted, nor by a mere show of detachment.
But as strength, stability, and inner freedom grow, so
  does Self-awareness grow.

Having realized the Self, the wise find satisfaction.
Their evolution complete, at peace and free from
  longing, they are at one with everything.

This supreme union is the goal of the Vedānta.
The wise, the unattached who live this state, are
  immortal and when they die remain united with
  the One.

At the time of death, smell, taste, sight, touch, and
  hearing dissolve into their deities, and the five
  prānas return to their source.
The individual's soul and all his deeds join with the
  supreme, the Immortal.

MUNDAKA UPANISHAD

As rivers flow into the sea, losing their individuality,
so the enlightened, no longer bound by name
and form, merge with the Infinite, the radiant
cosmic Being.

Truly, he who knows *brahman* becomes *brahman,* and
all his descendants become knowers of *brahman.*
He transcends suffering and the influence of evil.
Free from the chains of ignorance, he enjoys
immortality.

This knowledge may be taught only to those who
perform the rites, only to those who are learned
in the scripture, only to those who with
devotion surrender themselves, only to those
who are established in *brahman.*
To these alone and no one else."

This is the teaching of *brahman,* expounded in
ancient times by Angiras to Shaunaka.

All glory to the great seers!
Yes, all glory to the great seers!

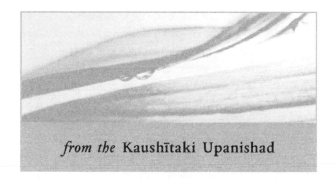

from the Kaushītaki Upanishad

INDRA, KING OF THE GODS, is the most hymned of the Vedic deities. Dwelling in the sumptuous City of Immortality, he represents power, action, victory, and all the virtues of vital youthfulness; his weapon is the invincible thunderbolt. But Indra has his weaknesses. While he never descends to the malign vindictiveness of his contemporary Jehovah, he is overly fond of pleasure, has a history of licentiousness, and displays considerable pride. As a result, his cosmic escapades frequently land him in trouble, reminding us that despite his exalted status, even the king of the gods is still confined to the relative world, which, bound by duality, is ever imperfect.

In the following passage, Indra's boasts soon develop into the lesson that we are all one Self. To do this, he first identifies himself with *prāna,* the life breath. As the universal force that animates all existence, *prāna* is similar to *chi* in Taoism, *ruach* in Judaism, and *pneuma* in Greek thought. In its highest expression, *prāna* is the dynamism inherent in the silent Absolute, its tendency to vibrate and become the creative energy that generates life. In shaping the world of duality, *prāna* becomes both intelligence and existence, mind and matter, subject and object.

In the graded series of highly sensitive energy fields that constitute the human individual, the stepping down of *prāna* is given different names according to the functions it assumes as it nourishes and enlivens the entire physiology. This is composed not only of the gross bodily structure known to Western medicine but also a second, subtle nervous system made of very refined material, often called the "subtle body" in esoteric teachings. Although this is imperceptible to conventional objective investigation, it is the basis of traditional Oriental health care systems, such as Ayurveda and acupuncture. This subjective nervous system links the gross anatomy with its abstract source, the pure intelligence of the Self, and acts as a filter through which the qualities of the Self are reflected. If the subtle nervous system is pure and unstressed, then the qualities of pure intelligence will naturally be displayed on the surface of our life. If, however, as is usually the case, the subtle levels of the individual are out of balance and blocked by the unresolved residue of past experience, then our natural happiness, freedom, and creativity will be compromised. If these imbalances are left untreated, they will eventually manifest on the gross level as illness.

The flow of *prāna* is quickened and strengthened through spiritual practice, which revitalizes the nervous system, flushes out those accumulated physical, psychological, and emotional impurities that are the legacy of aberrant life patterns, and gradually promotes a more benign neurochemistry.

As we evolve, more and more of our karmically seeded latent tendencies emerge into the daylight of conscious awareness, from where they can be purified and released—either by being transcended or by being acknowledged and, if necessary, acted out. Through this process of inner alchemy, the entire nervous system, gross and subtle, becomes progressively freed from its karmic dross and increasingly able to reflect the pure and luminous awareness that is the Self. Self-realization takes us beyond even the luminous realms of the gods who, from this point of view, represent stages of our own development yet to unfold.

Pratardana, the son of Devadāsa, servant of God, through courage and persistence attained the cherished realm of Indra, ruler of Heaven. On his arrival, the mighty Indra greeted him: "Pratardana, you may ask for any gift you wish."

Pratardana replied, "Please choose for me, O Lord. Give me whatever you think will be of the greatest benefit to mankind."

"A god does not make choices for a mortal," came the answer. "You must choose for yourself."

"If the choice is left to me, it can be no real gift," responded Pratardana.

So Indra, being Truth itself, remained faithful to his word, saying to Pratardana, "Then know me alone. This, indeed, I consider the best for mankind, that he should know me. For it was I who killed Vishvarūpa, the three-headed son of Tvashtri, the Weapon-Shaper. It was I who delivered the Arunmukhas, the dawn-faced ascetics, to the wolves. Breaking many pacts, I have killed so many demons: In the sky, I killed the followers of Prahlāda the demon king; in the air, I killed the hordes of Pauloma, whose daughter I then eloped with; and on earth, I killed those malign star-dwelling spirits, the Kālakanjas. And not a single hair of the body I had at those times was harmed! In the same way, he who knows me cannot be harmed, whatever he may do. Even if he steals, kills an unborn child, or even kills his mother or his father, whatever sin he commits, he does not pale with fear."

Then Indra continued: "For I am *prāna,* the breath of each day's life, the vitality in all beings. Glorify me; I am life and I am immortality. Life is breath and breath is life; for so long as there is breath in the body, there is life. From *prāna* comes the nectar of life, and as awareness *prāna* brings true understanding. He who glorifies me as the breath of life enjoys fullness in this life, and becomes indestructible, immortal even, in the heavenly realms after death.

"It is taught," he went on, "that each sense has its own intelligence, but actually each of these stem ultimately from the one *prāna.* Otherwise, how could the eyes see, how could the ears hear, how could the voice speak, or how could the mind think? These separate sense intelligences are all united in *prāna.* So when the voice speaks, it is Life itself speaking. When the eye sees, it is Life itself seeing. When the ear hears, it is Life itself hearing. When the mind thinks, it is Life itself thinking. And when the breath rises and falls, it is Life itself breathing.

"It is indeed so," continued Indra. "There is, moreover, something superior to these five sense intelligences. We can live without speech, for there are the dumb; we can live without sight, for there are the blind; we can live without hearing, for there are the deaf; we can live without thought, for there are the simple; and we can live without limbs, for there are the crippled. But we cannot live without breath. It is *prāna* alone, as the pure intelligence we call the Self, that informs and animates this body. So it is to *prāna* we should sing all hymns of praise. *Prāna* is the essence of the life breath. And what is the life breath? It is pure intelligence. And what is pure intelligence? It is the life breath."

III.1–3

And Indra continued further:
"When awareness governs speech, through speech
     one knows all names.
When awareness governs breath, through breath one
     knows all smells.
When awareness governs the eyes, through the eyes
     one knows all forms.

from the KAUSHĪTAKI UPANISHAD

When awareness governs the ears, through the ears
    one knows all sounds.
When awareness governs the tongue, through the
    tongue one knows all tastes.
When awareness governs the hands, through the
    hands one knows all action.
When awareness governs the body, through the body
    one knows pleasure and pain.
When awareness governs the genitals, through the
    genitals one knows joy, delight, and procreation.
When awareness governs the feet, through the feet
    one knows all movement.
When awareness governs the mind, through the
    mind one knows all thoughts.

For truly, without awareness speech would not
    reveal any name at all. We say: 'My mind
    was elsewhere; I did not notice that name.'
And without awareness breath would not reveal any
    smell at all. We say: 'My mind was elsewhere;
    I did not notice that smell.'
And without awareness the eyes would not reveal
    any form at all. We say: 'My mind was
    elsewhere; I did not notice that form.'
And without awareness the ears would not reveal

any sound at all. We say: 'My mind was
elsewhere; I did not notice that sound.'
And without awareness the tongue would not reveal
any taste at all. We say: 'My mind was elsewhere;
I did not notice that taste.'
And without awareness the hands would not reveal
any action at all. We say: 'My mind was
elsewhere; I did not notice that action.'
And without awareness the body would not reveal
any pleasure or pain. We say: 'My mind was
elsewhere; I did not notice that pleasure or pain.'
And without awareness the genitals would not reveal
any joy, delight, or procreation. We say: 'My
mind was elsewhere; I did not notice that joy,
delight, or procreation.'
And without awareness the feet would not reveal
any movement at all. We say: 'My mind was
elsewhere; I did not notice that movement.'
And without awareness the mind would not reveal
any thought at all. We say: 'My mind was
elsewhere; I did not notice that thought.'"

And Indra continued further:
"It is not just speech we should seek to understand,
we should know the one who speaks.

It is not just smells we should seek to understand,
    we should know the one who smells.
It is not just forms we should seek to understand,
    we should know the one who sees.
It is not just sounds we should seek to understand,
    we should know the one who hears.
It is not just tastes we should seek to understand,
    we should know the one who tastes.
It is not just activity we should seek to understand,
    we should know the one who acts.
It is not just pleasure and pain we should seek to
    understand, we should know the one who
    experiences.
It is not just joy, delight, and procreation we should
    seek to understand, we should know the one
    who enjoys.
It is not just movement we should seek to understand,
    we should know the one who moves.
It is not just thought we should seek to understand,
    we should know the one who thinks.

These ten elements of existence depend upon
    intelligence, and the ten elements of intelligence
    depend, in turn, upon existence.
For, truly, if there were no elements of existence
    there could be no elements of intelligence, and if

there were no elements of intelligence, there
could be no elements of existence.

From either on its own no form is possible.

But in truth, these ten elements constitute one
whole.

Just as in a wheel the sections of the rim are joined
to the spokes, and the spokes unite in the hub,
so these ten elements of existence join with ten
elements of intelligence, and these ten elements
of intelligence are united in *prāna*.

This same *prāna* is itself the knower — blissful,
timeless, and immortal.

Good deeds do not improve Him; evil does not
diminish Him.

He is the cause of right in those who rise, and the
cause of wrong in those who fall.

He is the sovereign and protector of the universe.

He is the lord of all.

'He is my Self!'—this you should know.

Yes, 'He is my Self!'—this you should know."

III.6–8

from the Katha Upanishad

THERE IS NO DEATH, only a change of worlds. Understood aright, life is the uninterrupted glory of the Divine, that eternal matrix of Consciousness in which apparently individuated beings appear, evolve, and eventually disappear, time after time. Until a born individual ceases to identify with the impermanent, separative ego personality and realizes this matrix to be the immortal Self, he or she will continue to suffer death and rebirth in the school of experience, like an actor who, never quite getting it right, has to return to the stage to play a different part, show after show.

Though death seems to most of us a fearsome and unfamiliar affair, we are constantly being educated in its ways, for our life is a continuous process of change, and each change is a little death survived. Not only do we live encircled by death, but to live is itself to die: From the moment of our birth, each breath we take inexorably draws our death nearer. Nevertheless, despite its constant proximity, death for most of us is the mightiest of challenges, and therefore Yama, King of Death, is depicted as a suitably awesome deity, the stern embodiment of retribution and the lord of cosmic justice. But Yama, "the Binder," also rules in the heart of life, for it is he who personifies the eternal law that keeps the universe in check, dispensing the appropriate result for each action and regulating all things without exception.

As the Lord of Death, Yama is also the master of immortality, the gateway to which is meditation. There are many similarities between meditation and death; indeed, the one can be seen as a preparation for the other. Both are windows to levels of existence other than the physical; both proceed through the gradual inversion of attention and the natural cessation of breathing; both are radical purifications that lead to greater freedom and ever higher levels of evolution. And in both the skill of letting go is crucial. This skill, actually the greatest secret in handling both embodied existence and its end, is not mere license in the name of some spurious "freedom," but the unforced reversal of extroverted attention that allows the mind happily to surrender the limitations of time and space that habitually bind it so tightly. Only by so doing can we gain that inner dimension that, as the very source of our vitality, enables us to enjoy living to the full while simultaneously remaining

from the KATHA UPANISHAD

anchored to something that suffers no change, no diminishment.

It is for this reason that before the decline of the monastic life destroyed its contemplative traditions, Christianity referred to meditation as *ars moriendi:* "the art of dying." Without a trace of morbidity, the anonymous fourteenth-century contemplative classic *The Cloud of Unknowing* counsels that those who are serious on the spiritual path must eventually "die to themselves, and lose the radically self-centered awareness of being, for it is our own limited self that stands in the way of God." Put simply, God can only come to call when "I" am not there.

According to an ancient Vedic story, Nāchiketas, the devout son of a poor brahmin, is dissatisfied with the gifts his father has offered to the sacrificial priests and insists that he be offered instead. Enraged, his father responds: "All right then, to Yama, the King of Death, I give you!"

Arriving at Yama's realm, Nāchiketas finds he is away roaming the world and has to wait, unfed, for three days and nights. Yama, on his return, grants the boy three wishes in recompense. Nāchiketas first chooses the gift of forgiveness, the ability to release his past by letting go of all he has held stored in his heart. His second wish is for the gift of inner fire,

that tenacious energy that will allow him to persevere
on the path of purification until its end. His third
wish is to know how the recurring cycle of death and
rebirth may be overcome and how that which is
immortal may be gained. The following passages are
part of the King of Death's reply.

Yama, King of Death, said:

"Let us light the fire of Nāchiketas, the purifying fire
whose flames, once kindled, are the bridge to
immortality.

And let us know the supreme imperishable *brahman,*
the fearless farther shore of life, the end of all
our seeking.

Now, imagine the Self as the rider in a chariot.

The body is the chariot, the intellect the driver, and
the mind the reins.

The senses are the horses and their objects are the
road.

When combined with the senses and the mind, the
Self becomes 'the Enjoyer'—so say those who
know.

When a man lacks wisdom his mind is always
restless, and his senses are wild horses dragging
the driver this way and that.

But when he has become wise his mind is collected,
and his sense-horses are tamed, obedient to the
driver's will.

He who lacks wisdom, whose mind is unsteady,
whose actions are not pure, such a one never
reaches the highest state and will suffer rebirth
again and again.

But he who is wise, whose mind is steady, who is
ever pure, such a one reaches the highest state,
from which there is no return.

He who has wisdom as his driver, and the reins of
his mind controlled, such a one reaches the end
of his journey, the supreme abode of Vishnu,
the all-pervading.

Subtler than the organs of perception are the
faculties of sense.
Subtler than them is the mind, filled with thoughts
and feelings.
Subtler than this is the intellect, which is the faculty
of choice.
Subtler than this is the ego, creating the sense
of 'I.'
Subtler than this is the underlying cause of all.
And subtler still is the Self, supreme and
universal.
There is nothing subtler than this.

from the KATHA UPANISHAD

This is the Absolute.
This is the end of all suffering.

Thus the Self lies hidden and is not openly
    displayed.
But It is known to those of subtle sight, whose
    vision is purified and clear.

The wise man's senses are governed by his mind.
His mind is governed by his intellect.
His intellect is governed by his active self.
And his active self is governed by the silent Self.

Wake up!
Seek the Truth!
Rise above ignorance!
Search out the best teachers, and through them find
    the Real.

But beware!
'The path is narrow,' the sages warn, 'sharp as a
    razor's edge, most difficult to tread.'"

1.III.2–14

And the Lord of Death continued:

"The pure Self cannot be found through studying
the Vedas, nor through learned argument, nor
through much hearing of the scriptures.
The Self is known only to those It chooses.
To them alone It reveals Its true nature.

The Self is not revealed to anyone whose ways have
not changed, whose senses are not still, whose
mind is not quietened, whose heart is not at
peace.

For who really knows what the Self is—the One to
whom priests and warriors are but food, and
death is but a sauce?"

1.II.23–25

"The Self is not to be seen, for It has no visible form.
Yet, when the mind becomes clear, and the heart
becomes pure, then can the Self be known.
And those who know It enjoy eternity.

When the five senses are stilled, and thinking has
ceased, when even the intellect does not stir,
then, say the wise, one has reached the highest
state.

from the KATHA UPANISHAD

This state, in which the senses are steady and at rest,
    is known as yoga, or union.
Now the attention is no longer distracted, for yoga
    is the end and the beginning of all.

Speaking, thinking, looking—none of these can
    reveal the Self.
It lies beyond the senses and can only be
    understood by him who knows 'It is.'

First accept that the Self exists, and accept that It
    can be known.
Then you will be prepared to experience Its real
    nature.

When all the heart's desires are exhausted,
    immortality is born and the limitless *brahman* is
    enjoyed—even while still in this body.

When all the knots of the heart have been released,
    then truly a mortal becomes immortal.
Thus is the teaching.

The heart has one hundred and one subtle energy
    channels.
One of these rises to the crown.

This channel is the path to that which is immortal;
the others lead but to lesser worlds.

The cosmic spirit shines constantly within the heart,
as a white light the size of a thumb.

It should be carefully extracted, as the stem of a
reed is steadily drawn from its sheath.
This is the Pure, the Eternal.
Yes, this is the Pure, the Eternal."

Nāchiketas received this teaching and the whole art
of meditation from the King of Death. Freed
from all impurities, and even from death itself,
he realized *brahman*.

And so may any other who knows this truth about
the Self.

1.VI.9–18

from the KATHA UPANISHAD

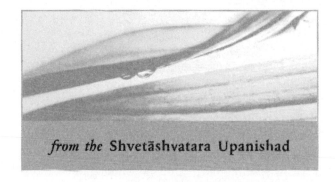

from the Shvetāshvatara Upanishad

1

IN THE WEST, polytheism is generally considered
a less evolved form of religion than monotheism.
But the trouble with conventional monotheism—the
worldview that champions the one god over and
against the many gods, "my God" as opposed to
"your gods"—is that it contains an unacknowledged
and destructive dualism. Such a perspective defines
itself by splitting off part of the whole into an
"other" that is different from itself. This "other" can
take multiple forms: It may be the many gods or
spiritual paths as opposed to the one "true" path or
god; the world and the flesh as opposed to the
spirit; or it can be the devil, the people who are not
chosen, the heathen, the infidel. Whatever its form,
the "other" is always inferior, a potential enemy to
be feared or despised, nullified by conversion, or, in
extreme cases, annihilated.

   The Upanishads do not subscribe to this antago-
nistic dualism, which, from their standpoint, stems

from a vestigial animism whereby the tribal group
always feels threatened by what is outside its territory
and appears different. Instead, they direct their vision
to the transcendental unity of that divine ground that
creates and sustains all diversity, including all the various deities, religions, and paths. From their perspective of Unity Consciousness they teach non-dualism
(*advaita*), a monism that, unlike conventional monotheism, sees all the gods as variegated aspects of the
undivided One. The many are no more a threat to
the One than the spectrum of colors is to pure white
light; in fact, they are its very expression. "What god
shall we worship?" rhetorically asks the eponymous
seer of the Shvetāshvatara. "Worship Him who is lord
of all the gods," comes the answer, "in whom the
whole creation rests." This text provides a moving and
poetic balance to other, more abstract Upanishads; it
is a lyrical and sustained hymn of praise to the One,
and to all its manifestations.

Just how the Absolute can assume the form of the
ever changing world and yet maintain its eternal and
unchanging status is something that has fascinated
theologians of all religions, and the sages of the
Upanishads were no exception. To explain this cosmic
sleight of hand, they described the relative world by
the concept of *māyā,* most famously propounded by

the great teacher Ādi Shankara and almost universally misunderstood ever since. *Māyā,* a very rich term, is usually translated as "illusion," but this is misleading. The word can be derived from the root *MĀ,* meaning "to make, limit, or divide," in which case it means "that which is made, limited, or divided," that is, the world of duality and distinctions. Because of our personal bias and projections, it is virtually impossible to say what the objective truth of any given situation really *is,* and in this sense our world is *māyā*—illusory, deceptive. This deceptiveness is especially pronounced in our time, when individual opinions are routinely championed and highly valued, despite the fact that they are generally influenced by media that are themselves compromised by the interests and prejudices of reporters, editors, and proprietors. In truth, nothing is really what it seems.

On another level, *mā* can mean "not" and *yā* "that"; hence *māyā* becomes "that which is not." This does not mean that the relative world has no existence; of course it undeniably does. But it has no *ultimate* reality, because it is impermanent and contingent. It exists, but from the standpoint of the Absolute, its existence has an elusive and mysterious, even dreamlike, quality. Moreover, as the Absolute remains transcendent even while manifest, the relative

"is not" the Absolute—it is only part of the whole—
in the same way that the waves "are not" the ocean.
For the enlightened person, the limited relative world
on its own is not the whole truth. The whole truth
is the luminous coexistence of both relative and
Absolute, in which all forms and phenomena are
seen to be nonbinding modifications of their unchanging source, simultaneously infinitely precious
and perfectly evanescent.

This ontological paradox was succinctly formulated by Shankara in his threefold proposition:
"*Brahman* is real; the world is unreal; *brahman* is the
world." Those who have interpreted his Advaita
Vedānta as a nihilistic dismissal of everyday reality
did not share his expanded level of consciousness.
Reduced to merely intellectual attempts to understand this subtlest of teachings, they did it grave
disservice by focusing only on the first two of his
statements while omitting the third.

A traditional story points up the dangers of trying
to imitate a higher level of consciousness without living it naturally. A student left the house of his teacher
having just received the supreme teaching that everything is a form of the formless God. Intoxicated by
this knowledge, he wandered out into the road, mar-
veling: "Oh, how wonderful! The trees are God, the

road is God, the fields are God, and I myself am God!" So absorbed was he that he failed to notice an elephant approaching. When at the last moment he did, his mood of bliss did not allow him to worry. "No matter!" he laughed as it bore down on him, "I am God, the elephant is God; God cannot injure God, let the elephant come!" The great beast duly knocked him flying and lumbered on its majestic way. Hearing the commotion, the teacher came out of his house to see his student picking himself up from the road, much the worse for wear. "What happened?" he asked. Dusting himself down, the student turned angrily on his teacher. "You told me that everything was God—the trees, the flowers, the animals, me myself—then how could this have happened?" he spluttered. "Yes," replied the teacher, smiling, "everything is indeed God—the trees, the flowers, you yourself. Even the elephant is God. But the elephant driver shouting at you to get out of the way, he too is God!"

"O *brahman,* You are One.

Though formless, through Your own power, and for Your own unfathomable purpose, You give rise to many forms.

You create the whole universe from Yourself, and, at the end of time, draw it back within Yourself.

O *brahman,* give us clear understanding.

You are Agni, the fire.
You are Āditya, the sun.
You are Vāyu, the wind.
You are Chandramas, the moon.
You are the brilliant stars.
You are Hiranyagarbha, the golden womb of all creation.
You are the cosmic waters.
You are Prajāpati, lord of all creatures.

You are woman.
You are man.
You are the youth.
You are the maiden
And You are the aged, tottering along with a stick.
Having taken form, You face in all directions.

from the SHVETĀSHVATARA UPANISHAD

You are the deep blue butterfly.
You are the parrot, green with red eyes.
You are the father of lightning.
You are the seasons and the seas.
Unborn, you are everywhere, and all that is, is born
    from You."

                                                    IV.1–.4

"Of what use are the Vedas to those who have not
        met that supreme eternal Being, from whom the
        Vedas come, and in whom the *devas* dwell?
Only those whose being flows with You find
        eternal joy.

For all the sacred texts, all the holy offerings, all the
        ceremonies, and all the rituals; the past, the
        present, and the future; all the Vedas speak of
        and this whole universe are but projections of
        You, imperishable *brahman,* conjured up by Māyā,
        the mother of illusion.
And through the art of Māyā, we are charmed by
        her creations.
Know that all of Nature is but a magic theatre, that
        the great Mother is the master magician, and that
        this whole world is peopled by her many parts.

You are the source of every source, from whom all
this emerges, and into whom this all returns.

You are the powerful one, the great benefactor,
resplendent and adorable, in whom we find
unending peace.

You who are creator and sustainer of the gods, the
ruler of all, Rudra, destroyer of ignorance, the
great seer, witness to the birth of the golden
womb, we beg of you clear sight.

What god should we worship?

Worship Him who is lord of all the gods, in whom
the whole creation rests, He who governs both
man and beast.

By knowing Him who is subtler than the subtlest,
the still center of all activity, the fashioner of
forms, enfolding the universe in His embrace, by
knowing Him as Love, we find eternal peace."

IV.8–14

"Whoever lives in the world of change, the world of
the three *gunas,* acts for the sake of action's fruits,
and by these fruits is bound to act again.

from the SHVETĀSHVATARA UPANISHAD

Life after life, the soul assumes new forms, according
to its qualities, and thus embodied reaps its due
reward.

Linked with ego and desires, the soul appears as a
light the size of a thumb.
But when linked with the Self and discrimination,
it shines like the point of a pin.

Know the soul to be only the hundredth part of the
hundredth part of the tip of a hair.
Yet within it lies the limitless expanse.

It is not female; it is not male; it is not neuter.
Yet, in assuming a body, the soul takes on such forms.

Through the spell of seeing, desiring, touching, and
uniting, a soul is born once more.
Through food and drink it grows.
And, depending on its deeds, it is reborn again.

According to its qualities, a soul takes many forms.
Some are coarse and some are fine, for the body it
assumes is shaped by its own tendencies."

V.7–12

The six orthodox systems of Indian philosophy describe reality from different levels of consciousness, culminating in Vedānta, the teaching of Unity. Sānkhya, the system that enumerates the constituent aspects of life as seen from the perspective of Cosmic Consciousness, divides the cosmos into two complementary principles: the spiritual *Purusha,* "the Person," and the material *Prakriti,* "Nature." He is Consciousness, the subjective aspect of life and the transcendental basis of mind; She is the primal substance of existence, the undifferentiated matter-energy from which the entire creation arises. Together they constitute one Life.

Prakriti is composed of three qualities known as *gunas* (literally: "strands of a rope")—*rajas, tamas,* and *sattva.* These are three basic tendencies inherent in all creation and are associated with the Hindu deities Brahmā, Shiva, and Vishnu. The undifferentiated *prakriti* is the equilibrium of the *gunas;* when this is disturbed the universe takes form and in every level of creation one or another of the *gunas* predominates.

Rajas is the dynamic, progressive, and creative influence, the centrifugal force similar to the *yang* of

Chinese thought, while *tamas,* the retarding influence
that checks *rajas,* is associated with the dark, cen-
tripetal force similar to *yin. Sattva* is the sustaining
influence that integrates, balances, and harmonizes
the other two. On another level, the three *gunas* can
be understood as the universal states of motion, mass,
and light.

Something in which *sattva* dominates will tend
to show the qualities of peace, purity, and stability,
whereas a dominance of the other two will result in
excessive passion or dullness. The best way to increase
sattva is meditation; the life of a yogi is traditionally
held to be the sattvic human ideal.

"Change, say some of the learned, is just the nature
of things.
Others say it is but the mark of time.
Yet they are all deluded, O radiant Lord, for it is by
Your own greatness that the wheel of the world
revolves.

This whole world is floating in You.
You are the highest intelligence, the master of the
gunas, and the maker of time.
You know all.
It is under Your command that Your own creation
unfolds—space and air and fire and water and
earth in turn evolve.

Having created the world, You take Your rest again.
You are united with the elements, and You are
united with the One.
From the One are born Purusha, the cosmic Spirit,
and Prakriti, mother of Nature.
From these two are born the *gunas,* which in turn
give birth to the objective world of space, air,

from the SHVETĀSHVATARA UPANISHAD

fire, water, and earth, and the subjective world of
ego, intellect, and mind.
You are united with Time, and the subtleties of man.

Without the *gunas* there can be no creation; by using
them You have formed everything that is.
And yet, You stand apart—even when dissolving all
that You have made.

You are the seed of all, the source of primal urging.
You are beyond past, present, and future.

You are undivided.
You are the adorable God of many forms.
You are the origin of all, awake within our very
minds.

Beyond the branching tree of life, beyond all time
and form, You are the one from whom all this
evolves, bringer of good and banisher of evil,
lord of power.

May we know You as our own Self, the
imperishable support of all.
May we know the Lord of lords, most brilliant of
the deities, Master of the masters, the Highest.

May we know You, the most adorable God, O Lord
of the universe.

We cannot see You acting, nor know Your means
of action.
Nowhere can we find Your better, nor even Your
equal.
Your mighty power is legion.
Your nature is intelligence and strength.

None can be Your master.
No one is Your lord.
Never can an image capture You.
You rule the rulers of the senses, yet You have
neither ruler nor creator.

O Lord, who has woven the web of the world from
Yourself, as a spider spins its threads, lead us to
freedom!

You are the one God, hidden in all.
You are everywhere, the inner Self of all, the seer of
deeds, dwelling in all, the uninvolved witness,
knowing all, pure Consciousness, free of all
qualities.

from the SHVETĀSHVATARA UPANISHAD

Remaining still, You are the Mover of everything
that moves.
You make the one seed many.
The wise know You as their own Self; to them, and
no one else, belongs eternal bliss.

You are the Eternal among eternals, the
Consciousness within all minds, the One within
the many, the end of all desiring.
When You are fully known, all limits are dissolved.

You are not lit by the light of the sun, nor by the
light of the moon, nor by stars, nor by lightning,
and much less still by fire.
It is only through Your brilliance that all these others
shine; it is by Your light this Universe is lit.

The one 'I AM' at the heart of creation, You are the
light of life.
Only by knowing You can we conquer death; there
is no other way.

You who have fashioned all forms from Yourself, the
knower of all, the one intelligence, the father of
time, the font of all qualities, the ruler of both
Purusha and Prakriti, the lord of the *gunas*.

It is You, spinning the wheel of life and death, who
shapes both suffering and its end.

You are That, extending everywhere, eternally
resplendent in Your glory, pure Consciousness,
the protector of all.
You rule this world forever.
How could there be any other ruler but You?

To You, who in the beginning created Brahmā, and
revealed to him the timeless Vedas, to You alone
I turn, longing for liberation.
To You, who through Your grace, allows Yourself to
be known.
You are the One: still, peaceful, blameless, pure, the
surest bridge to immortality, the fire that
consumes all suffering.

A man could more easily roll up the sky like a
length of cloth than he could end his suffering
without turning to You."

Through the power of meditation and the grace of
God, the wise Shvetāshvatara spoke the truth
about *brahman*.
He spoke to the most advanced students of the pure,
the supreme.

from the SHVETĀSHVATARA UPANISHAD

He spoke of what is pleasing to the company of
  seers.

This supreme secret of Vedānta, which was taught
  in earlier times, should not be revealed to him
  who is not at peace, nor to him who is not a
  son or a pupil.

To him who has the highest love for God, and for
  the guru as for God, to that great soul the truths
  taught here shine forth in all their glory.
Yes, to that great soul the truths taught here shine
  forth in all their glory!

Settle into peace, settle into peace, settle into peace."

VI.1–24

ALISTAIR SHEARER received an M.A. in Sanskrit and Indian studies from Lancaster University after doing an M.A. in literature at Cambridge. As a cultural historian specializing in India and Southeast Asia, he has lectured on the subject for many prestigious institutions, including London University, the British Museum, the Royal Academy of Arts, the Prince of Wales' Architectural Institute, the Tate Gallery, and the auction houses Christie's and Sotheby's. He currently divides his time between lecturing, teaching meditation courses, and leading cultural tours to the Indian subcontinent (www.trishulatravel.com). He has published ten books on the area, covering iconography, architecture, religion, philosophy and travel, the most recent of which is *The Yoga Sutras of Patanjali.*

PETER RUSSELL is one of the more revolutionary futurists and has been a keynote speaker at many international conferences in Europe, Japan, and the United States. His multi-image shows and videos, *The Global Brain* and *The White Hole in Time,* have won praise and prizes from around the world. In 1993 the environmental magazine *Buzzworm* voted Peter Russell "Eco-Philosopher Extraordinaire" of the year. He is the author of *The TM Technique, The Global Brain Awakens, Waking Up in Time,* and *From Science to God.* He divides his time between England and Sausalito, California.

DATE D